METHOD MAN

CONCEPT BY *METHOD MAN*
ILLUSTRATIONS BY *SANFORD GREENE*
SCRIPT BY *DAVID ATCHISON*
DESIGN BY *ROB HAYNES*
TONES BY *KELSEY SHANNON*
CREATIVE CONSULTATION BY *SHAUNA GARR*

SPECIAL THANKS TO:
JOHN CAUSEY
ANTONIO BOYD

G
C
GRAND CENTRAL
PUBLISHING

This book is a work of fiction. The dialogue and every scene and situation are fictitious. All characters who appear in this book are inventions, and not intended to resemble any real persons or events.

Grand Central Publishing
Hachette Book Group USA
237 Park Avenue
New York, NY 10017

Visit our Web site at www.HachetteBookGroupUSA.com.

Printed in the United States of America

First Edition: July 2008
10 9 8 7 6 5 4 3 2 1

Grand Central Publishing is a division of Hachette Book Group USA, Inc.
The Grand Central Publishing name and logo is a trademark of Hachette Book Group USA, Inc.

Library of Congress Control Number: 2008923308

ISBN-10: 0-446-69972-1
ISBN-13: 978-0-446-69972-3

Book production by Mada Design, Inc.

METHOD MAN

PROLOGUE

PRIVATE INVESTIGATOR PEERLESS POE TAKES THE CASES NO ONE ELSE WILL BECAUSE THOSE ARE THE ONLY CASES HE CAN GET. HIS CLOTHES NEED IRONING, HIS BREATH REEKS OF BOOZE AND HIS OFFICE STINKS OF MARIJUANA. AND HE WOULDN'T HAVE IT ANY OTHER WAY.

PEERLESS IS A DIRECT DESCENDANT OF CAIN, THE WORLD'S FIRST MURDERER. FOR HIS TRANSGRESSIONS, CAIN AND HIS DESCENDANTS BEAR THE MARK OF CAIN, A BIRTHMARK THAT ATTRACTS SUPERNATURAL PHENOMENA. TO ATONE FOR CAIN'S SINS, HIS DESCENDANTS MUST HUNT AND SLAY ABHORRENTS, CREATURES LEFT FROM THE EARLY DAYS OF CREATION: NEPHILIM, ROGUE SPIRITS, GIANTS, GOLEMS, LEVIATHANS, AND ANYTHING ELSE THAT COMES THEIR WAY.

THOUGH A NORMAL MAN WOULD NOT BE UP TO SUCH A TASK, PEERLESS IS NO ORDINARY MAN. LIKE HIS ANCESTORS, HE POSSESSES THE WRATH OF CAIN: A BERSERKER RAGE THAT INCREASES THE BEARER'S FEROCITY, PHYSICAL PROWESS, AND HEALING ABILITIES.

AS CAIN'S DESCENDANTS GREW IN NUMBER THEY FORMED THE ORDER OF THE SACRED METHOD TO HUNT DOWN AND ELIMINATE THE ABHORRENTS. THE METHOD MEN ARE A NEAR-FANATICAL RELIGIOUS ELITE ORDER OF DISCIPLINED MURDER-PRIESTS WHO USE THEIR ABILITIES TO ATTACK UNHOLY THREATS ON A GLOBAL SCALE. THOUGH A SKILLED METHOD MAN, PEERLESS'S PERSONAL PHILOSOPHY CONFLICTED WITH THE ORDER'S IDEOLOGY.

NOW PEERLESS WORKS AS A FREELANCE PRIVATE INVESTIGATOR, CONTINUING THE LABOR OF THE ORDER ON HIS TERMS AND AT HIS PRICE.

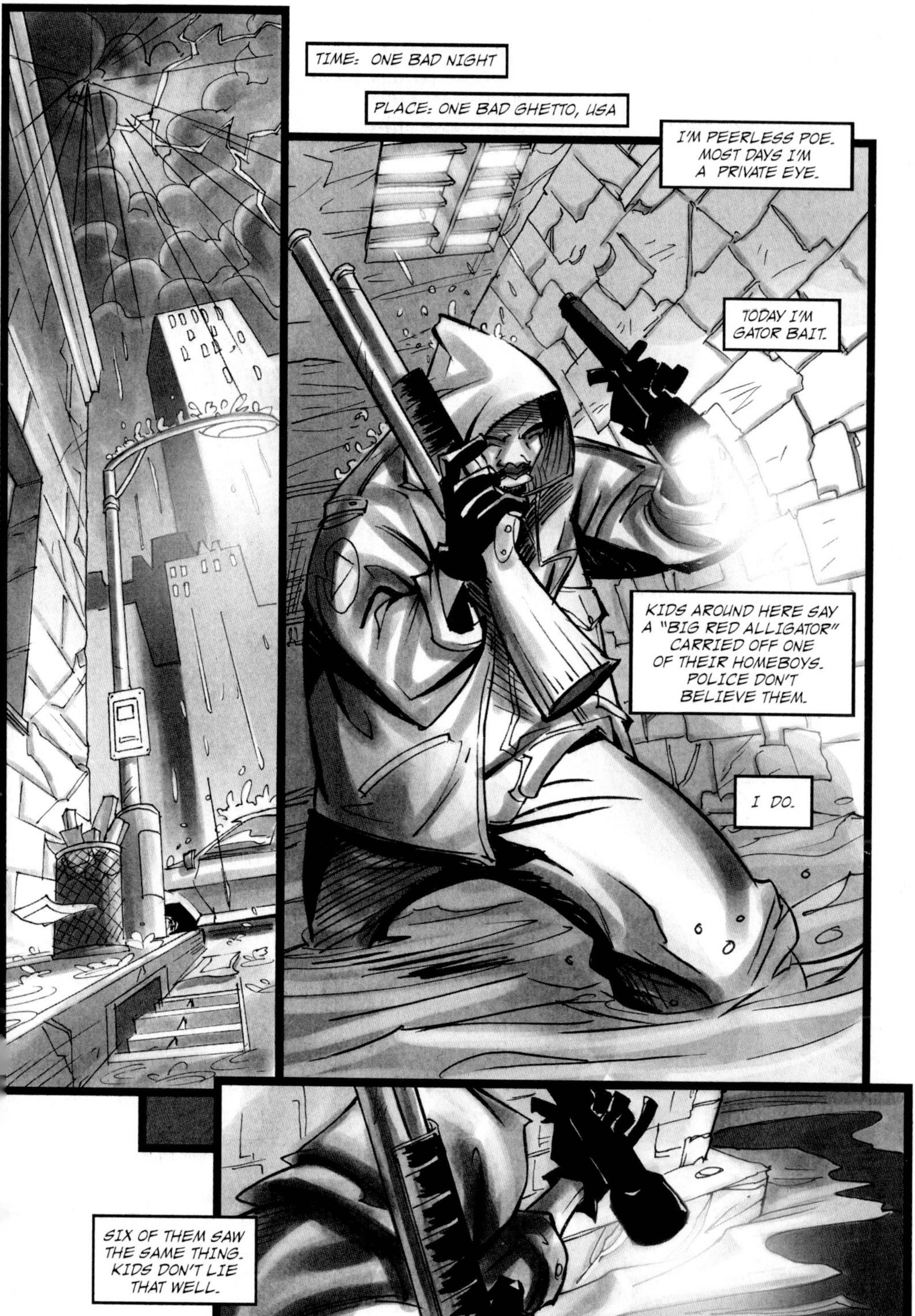
TIME: ONE BAD NIGHT
PLACE: ONE BAD GHETTO, USA
I'M PEERLESS POE. MOST DAYS I'M A PRIVATE EYE.
TODAY I'M GATOR BAIT.
KIDS AROUND HERE SAY A "BIG RED ALLIGATOR" CARRIED OFF ONE OF THEIR HOMEBOYS. POLICE DON'T BELIEVE THEM.
I DO.
SIX OF THEM SAW THE SAME THING. KIDS DON'T LIE THAT WELL.

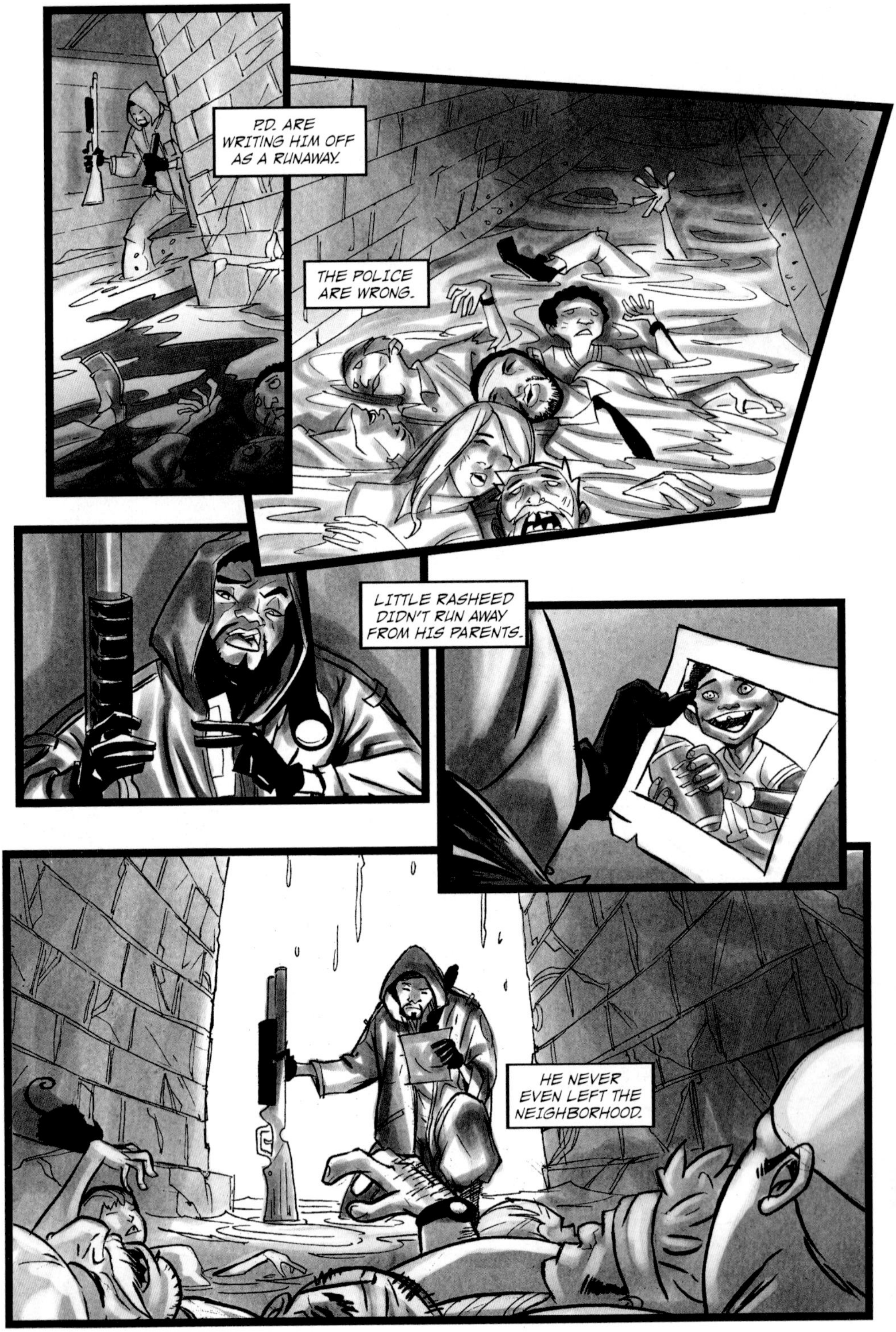
P.D. ARE WRITING HIM OFF AS A RUNAWAY.
THE POLICE ARE WRONG.
LITTLE RASHEED DIDN'T RUN AWAY FROM HIS PARENTS.
HE NEVER EVEN LEFT THE NEIGHBORHOOD.

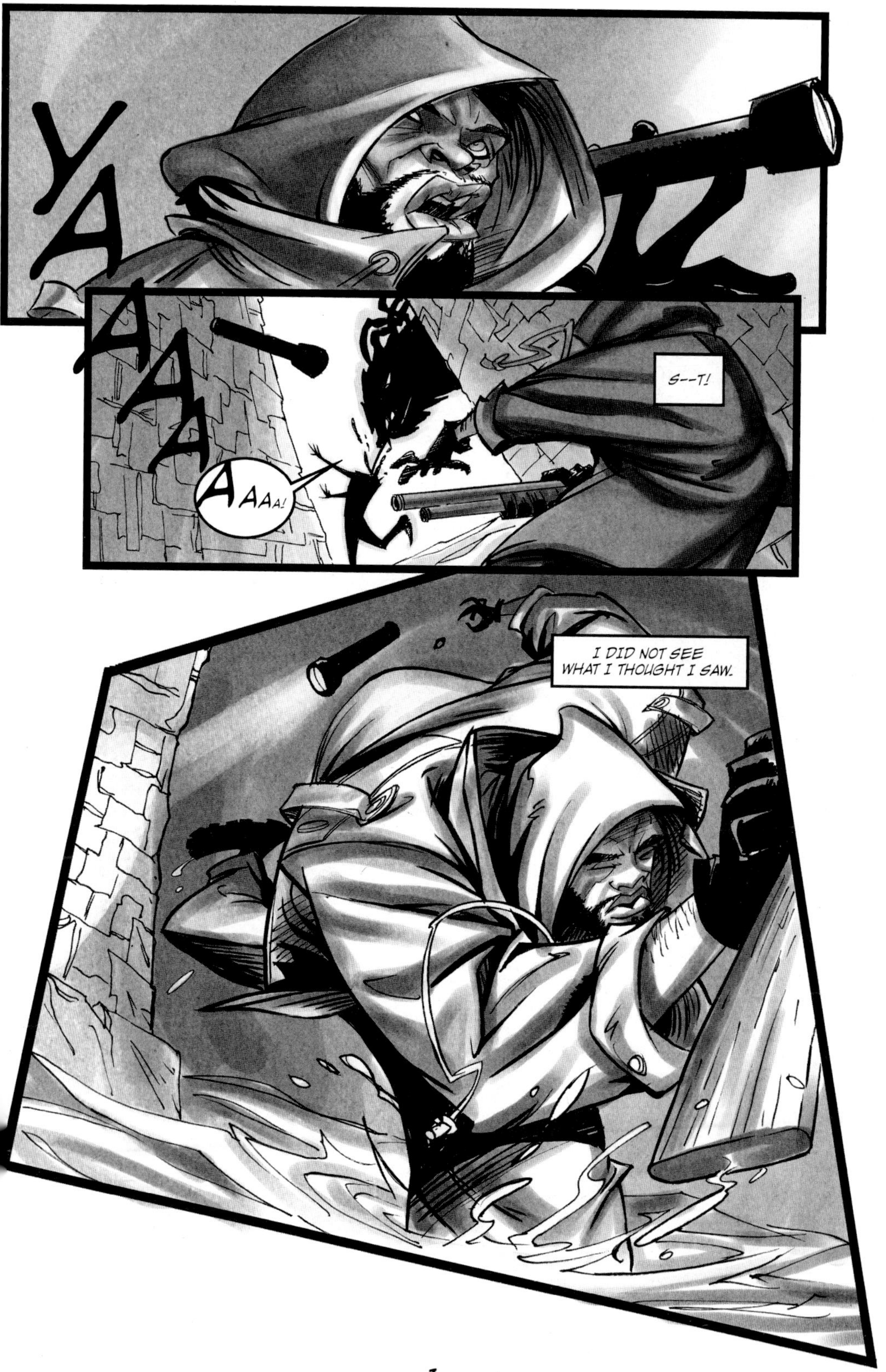
YAAAAA
AAAA!
S--T!
I DID NOT SEE WHAT I THOUGHT I SAW.

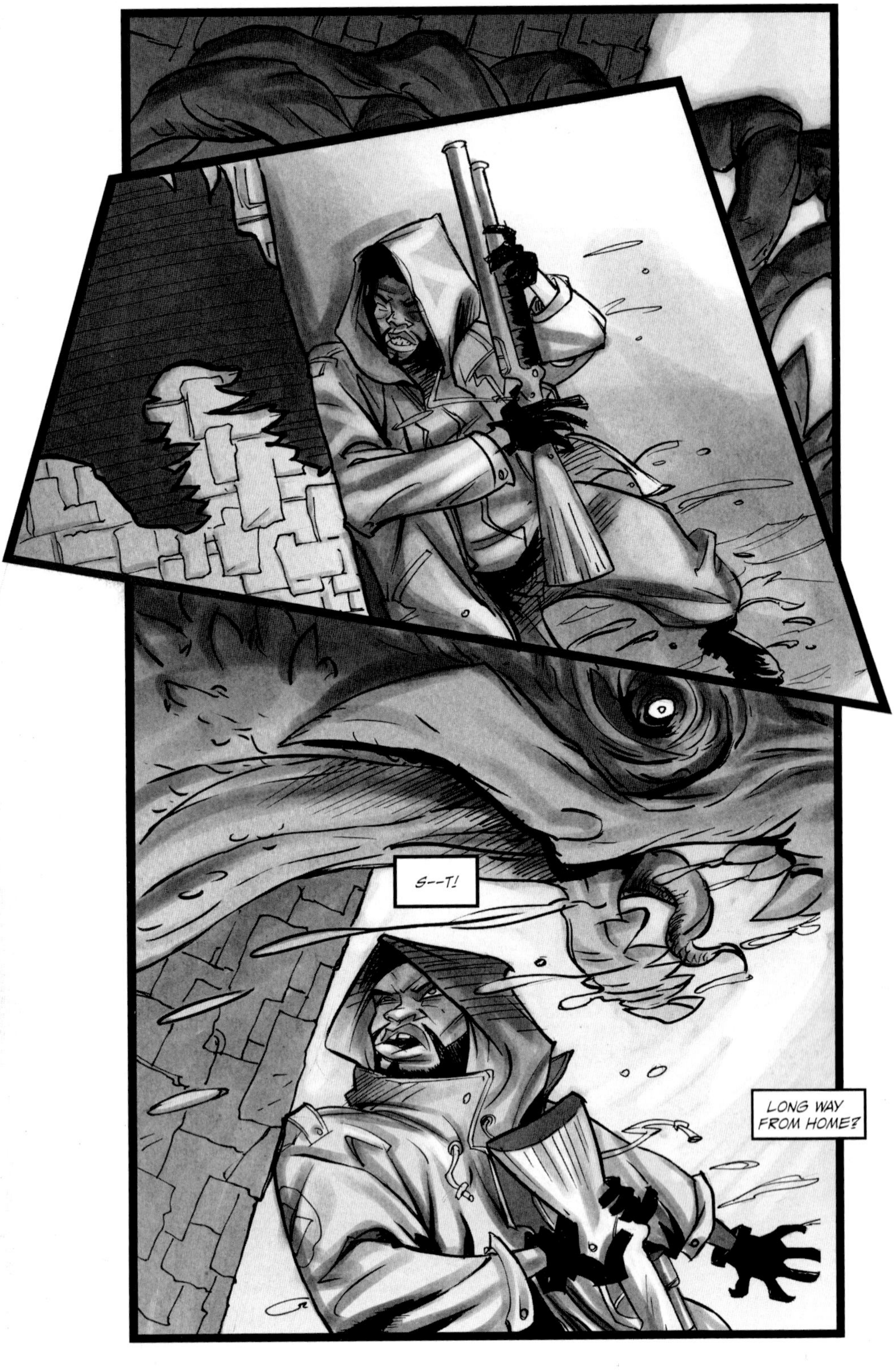
S--T!
LONG WAY FROM HOME?

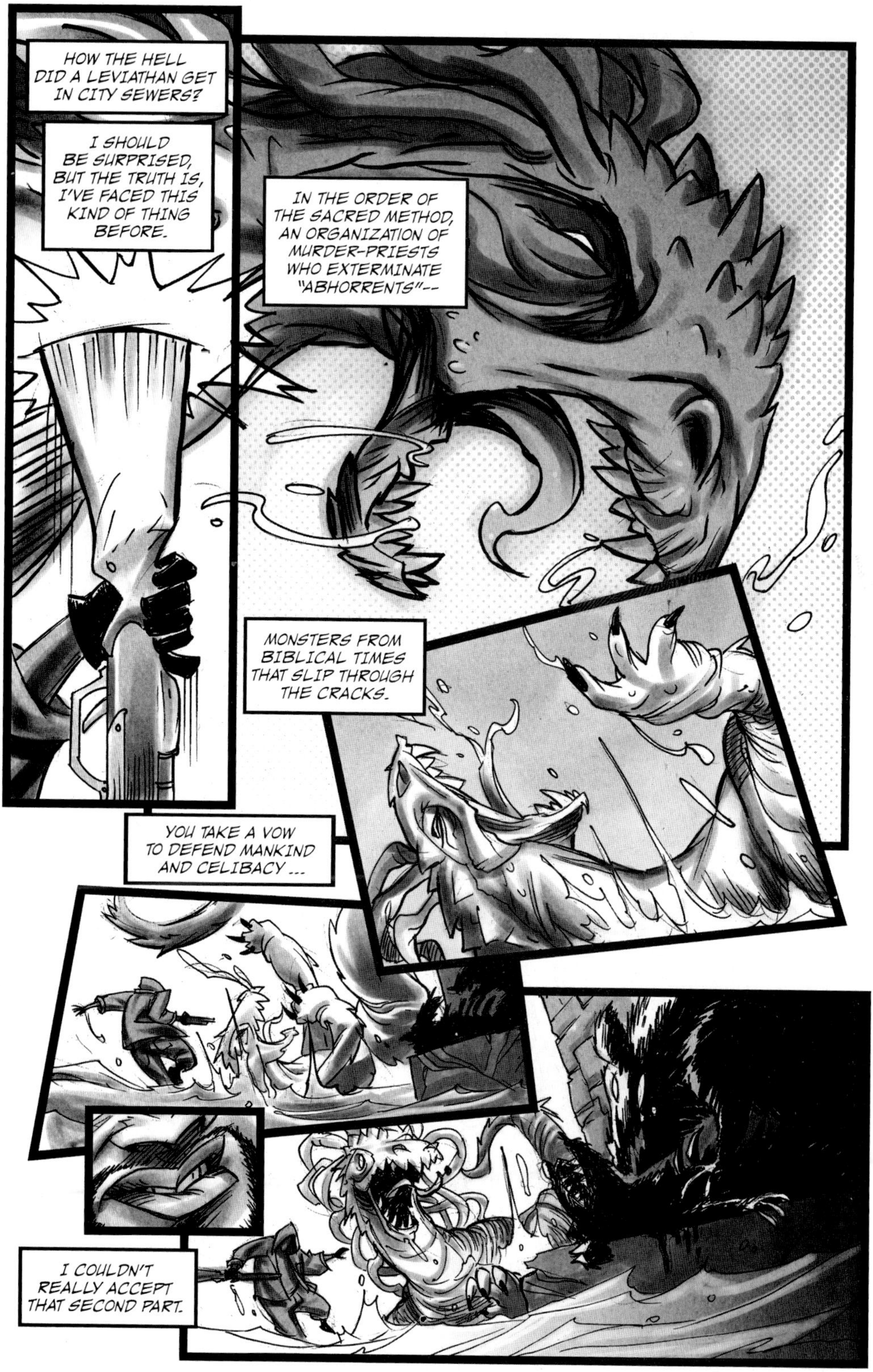
HOW THE HELL DID A LEVIATHAN GET IN CITY SEWERS?
I SHOULD BE SURPRISED, BUT THE TRUTH IS, I'VE FACED THIS KIND OF THING BEFORE.
IN THE ORDER OF THE SACRED METHOD, AN ORGANIZATION OF MURDER-PRIESTS WHO EXTERMINATE "ABHORRENTS"--
MONSTERS FROM BIBLICAL TIMES THAT SLIP THROUGH THE CRACKS.
YOU TAKE A VOW TO DEFEND MANKIND AND CELIBACY ...
I COULDN'T REALLY ACCEPT THAT SECOND PART.

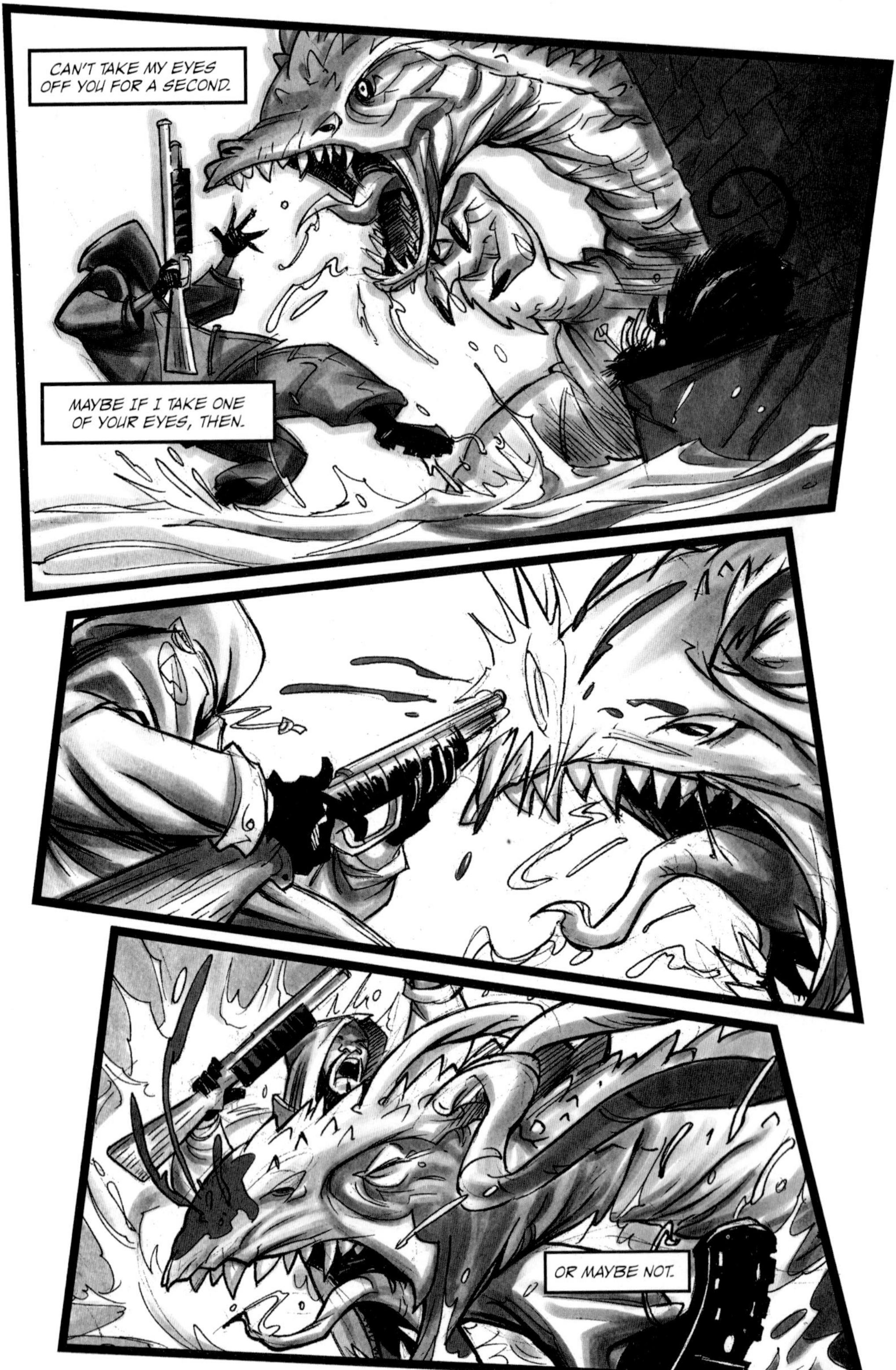
CAN'T TAKE MY EYES OFF YOU FOR A SECOND.
MAYBE IF I TAKE ONE OF YOUR EYES, THEN.
OR MAYBE NOT.

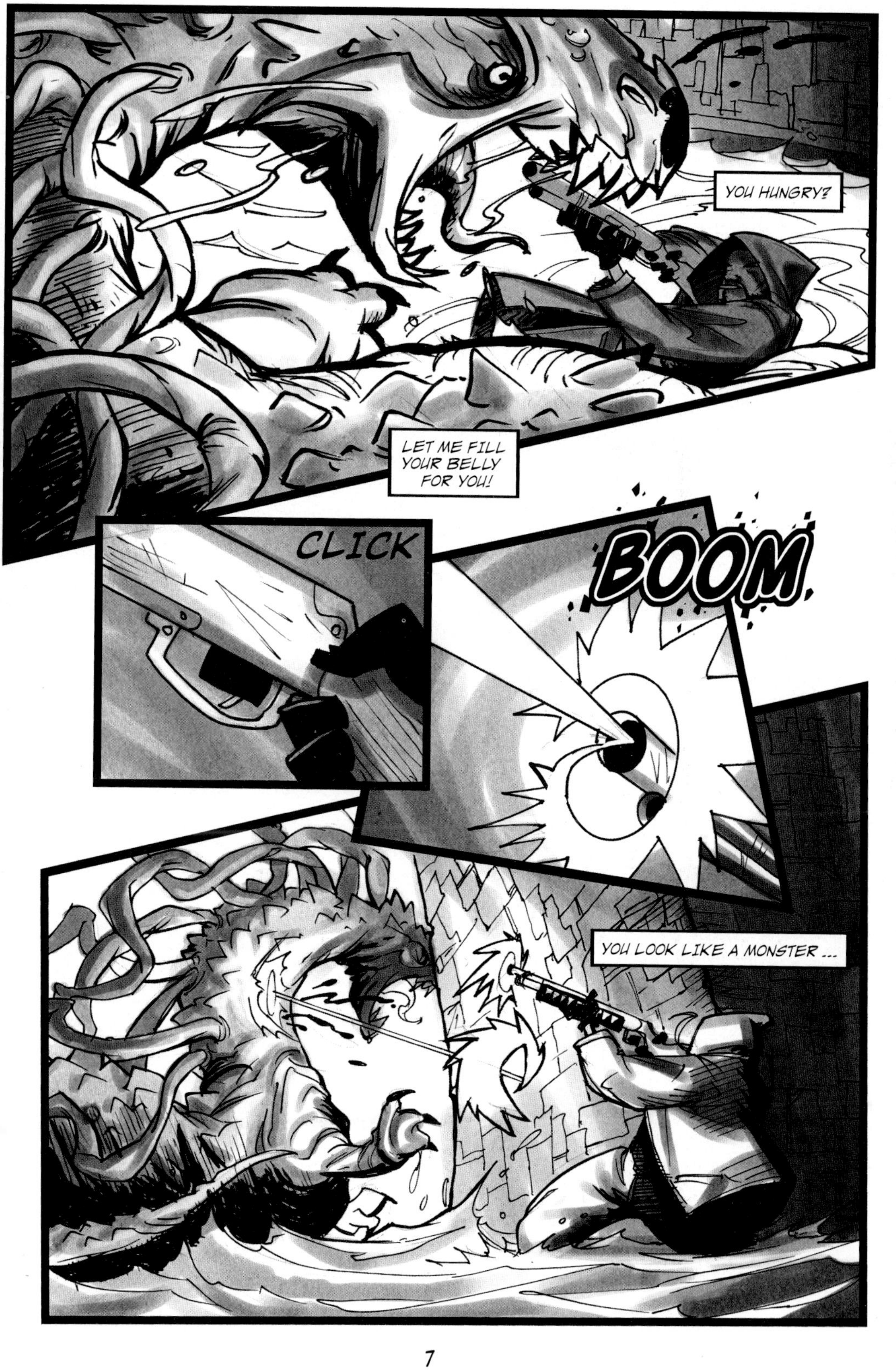
YOU HUNGRY?
LET ME FILL YOUR BELLY FOR YOU!
CLICK
BOOM
YOU LOOK LIKE A MONSTER ...

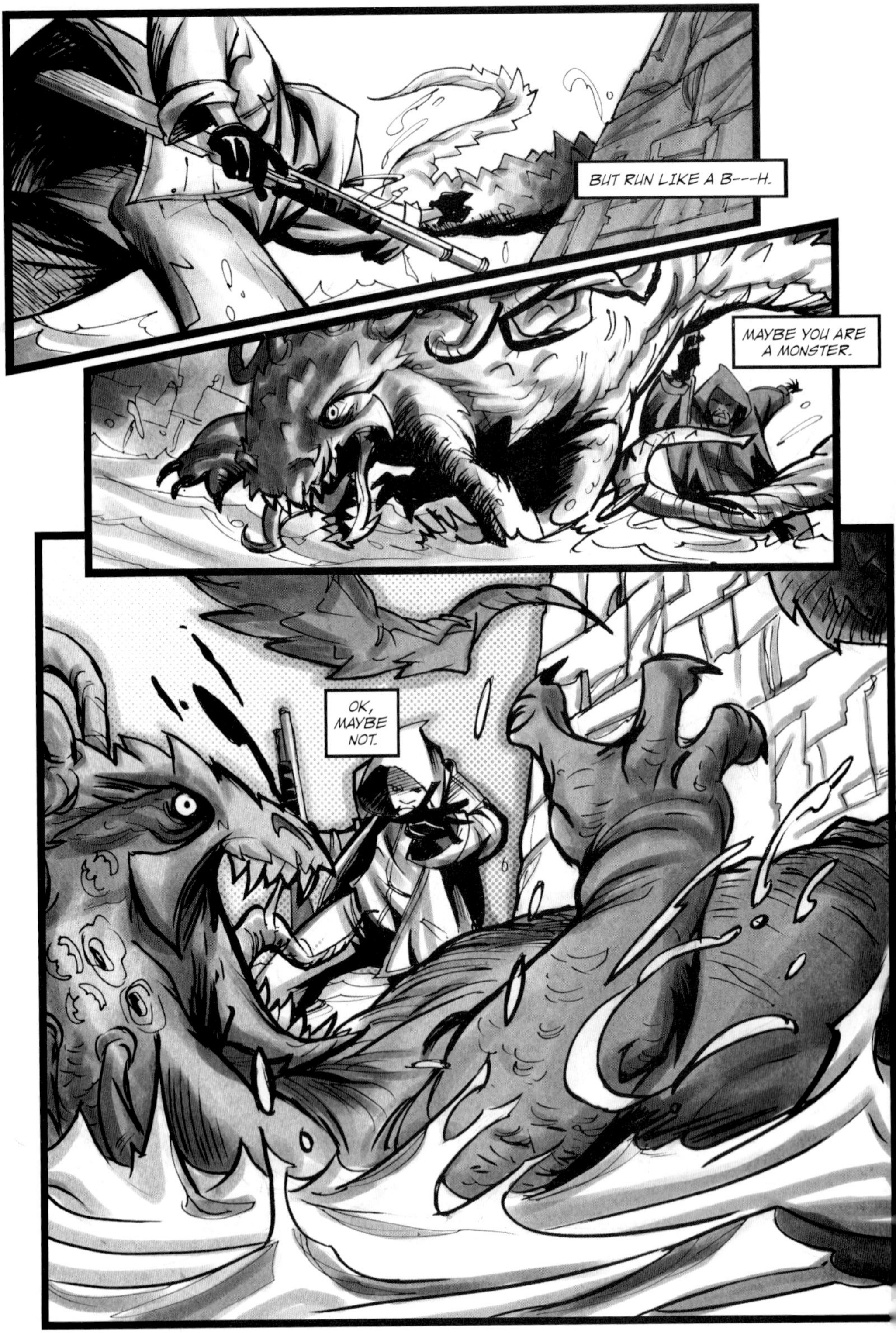
BUT RUN LIKE A B---H.
MAYBE YOU ARE A MONSTER.
OK, MAYBE NOT.

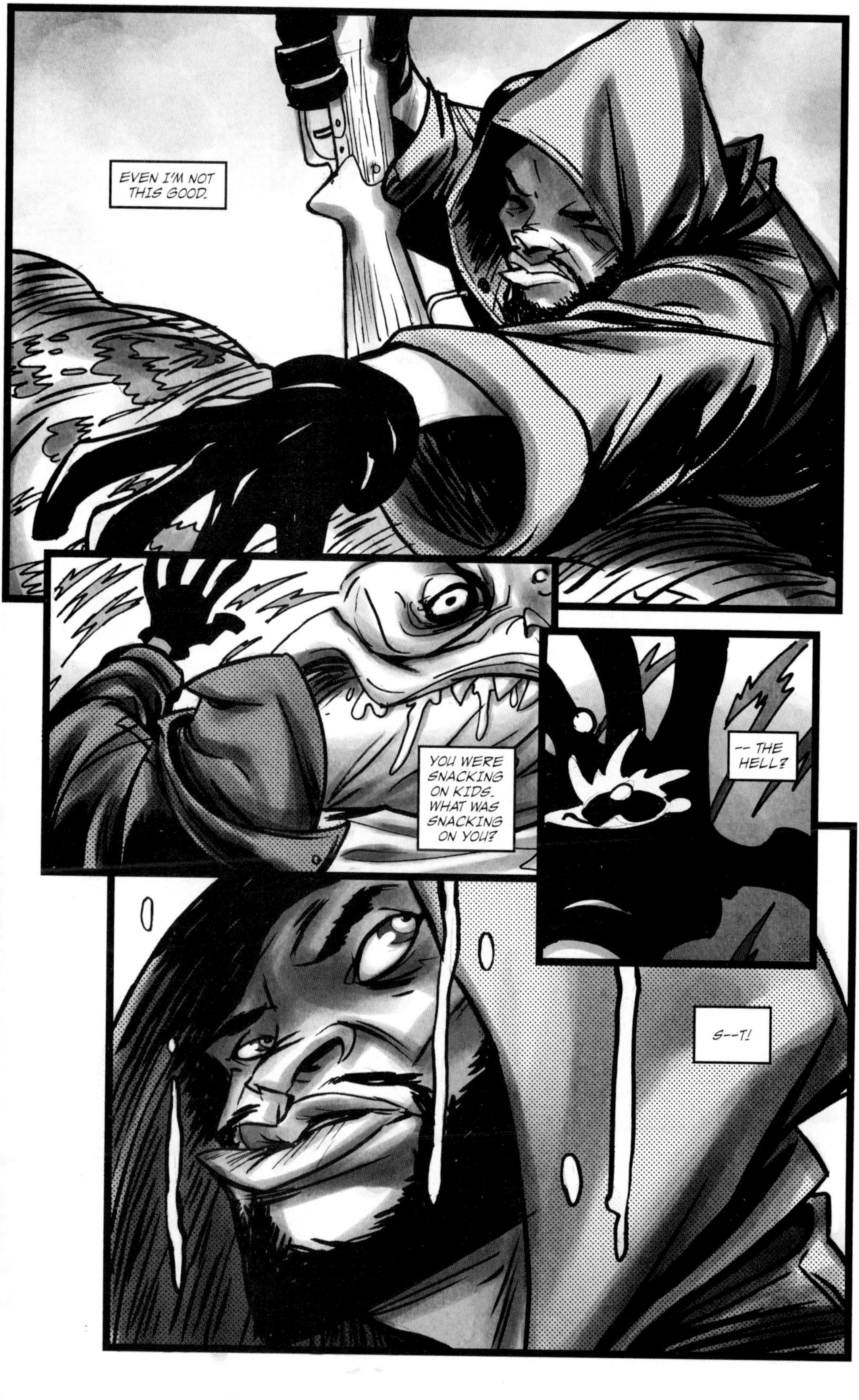
EVEN I'M NOT THIS GOOD.
YOU WERE SNACKING ON KIDS. WHAT WAS SNACKING ON YOU?
-- THE HELL?
S--T!

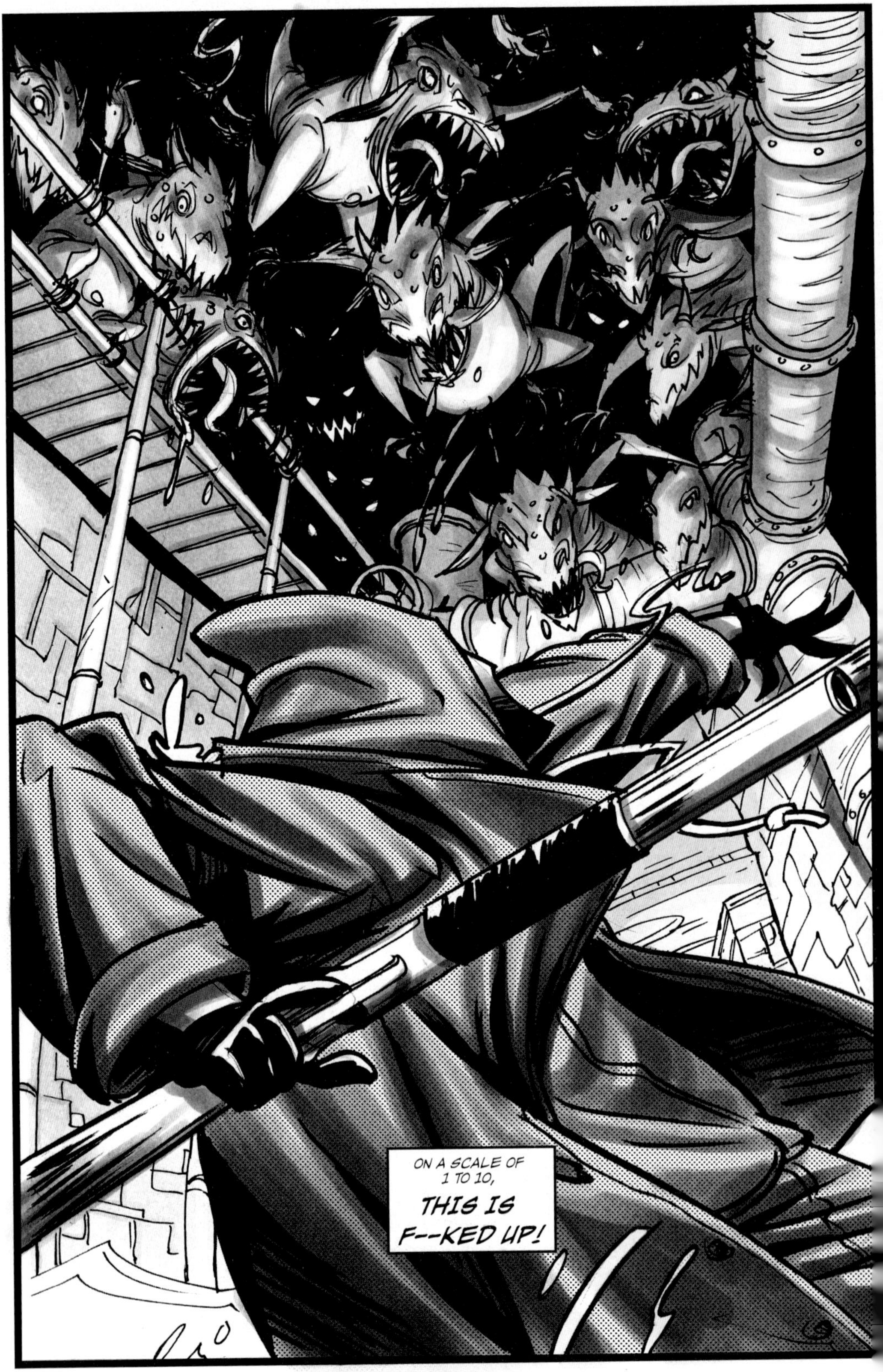
ON A SCALE OF
1 TO 10,
THIS IS
F--KED UP!

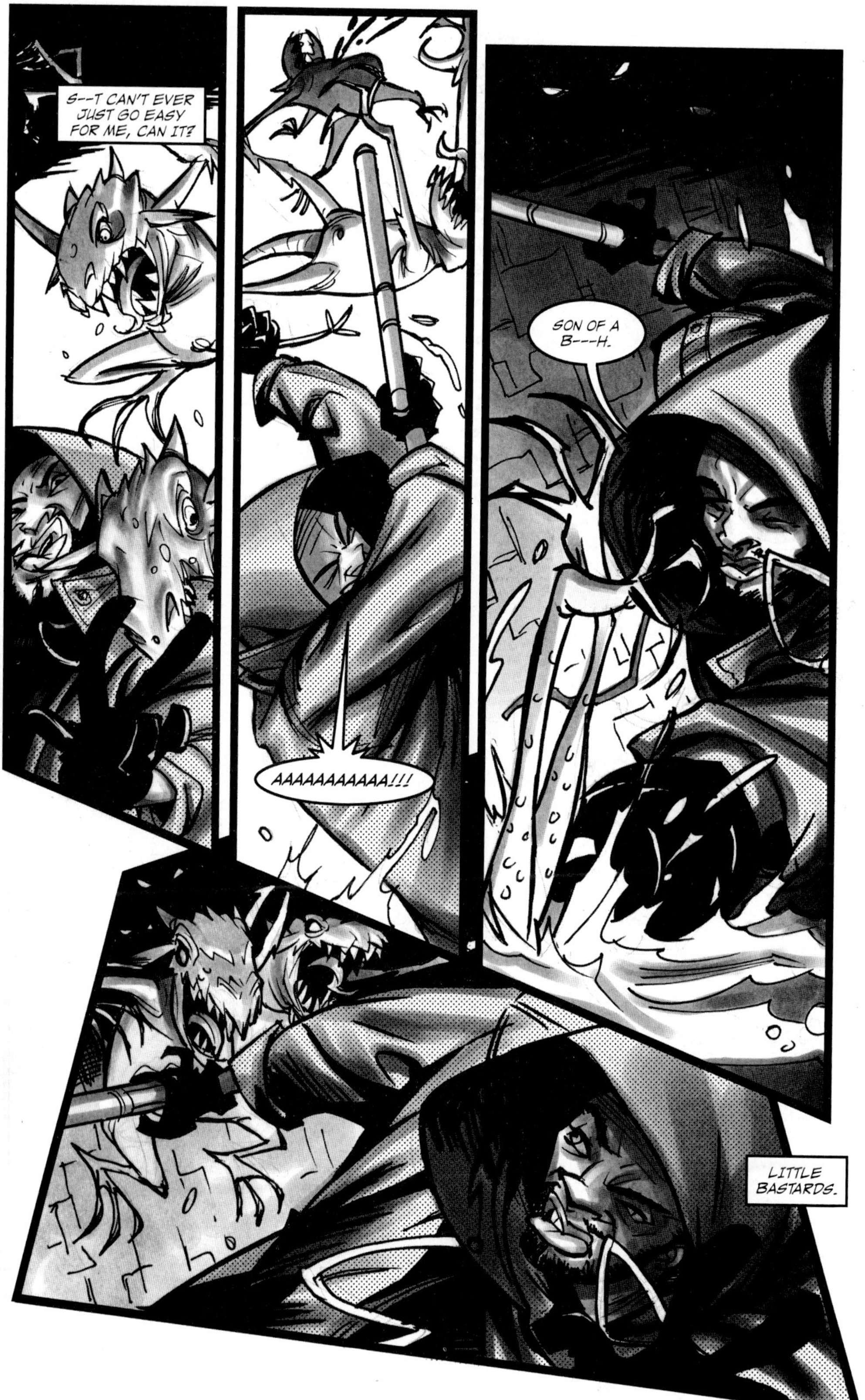
S--T CAN'T EVER JUST GO EASY FOR ME, CAN IT?
AAAAAAAAAAA!!!
SON OF A B---H.
LITTLE BASTARDS.

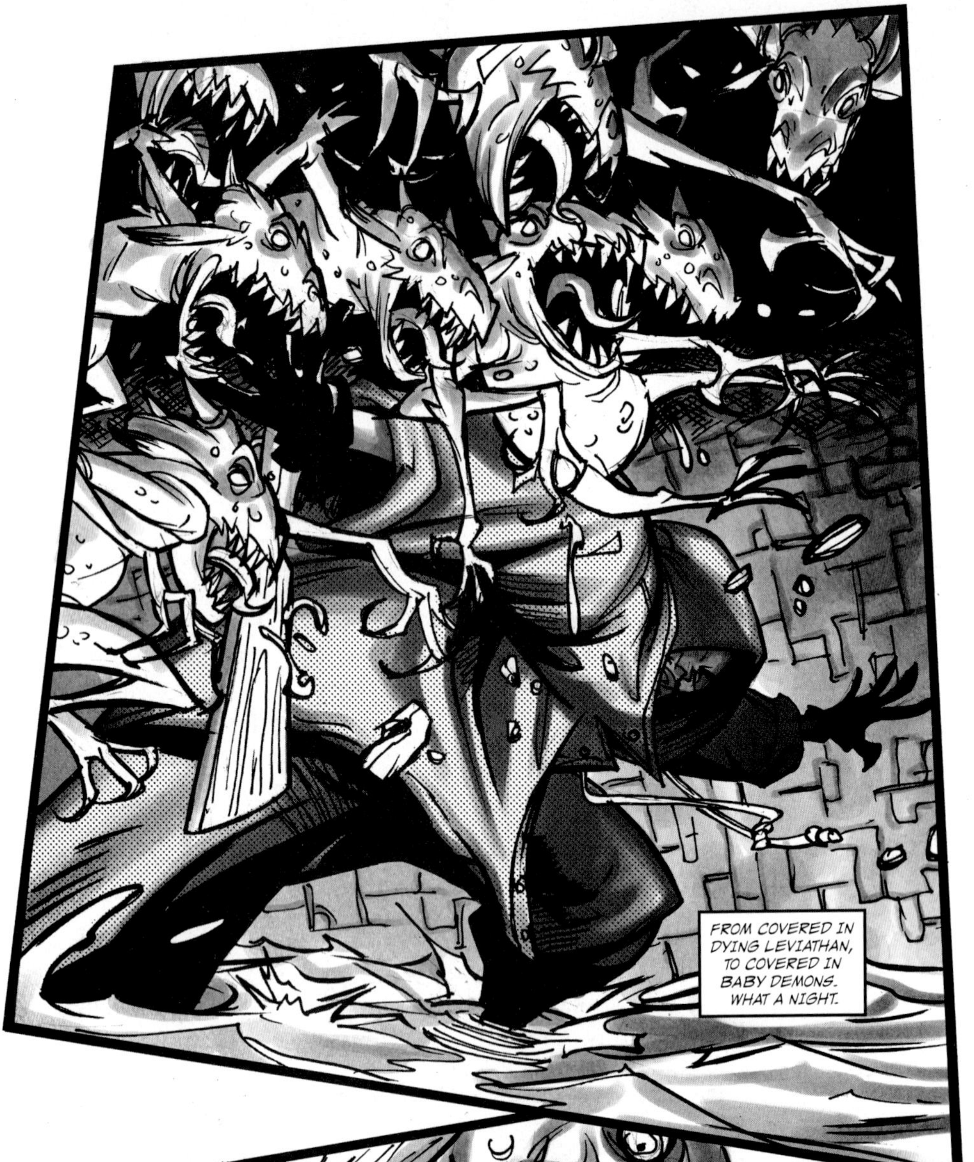
FROM COVERED IN DYING LEVIATHAN, TO COVERED IN BABY DEMONS. WHAT A NIGHT.

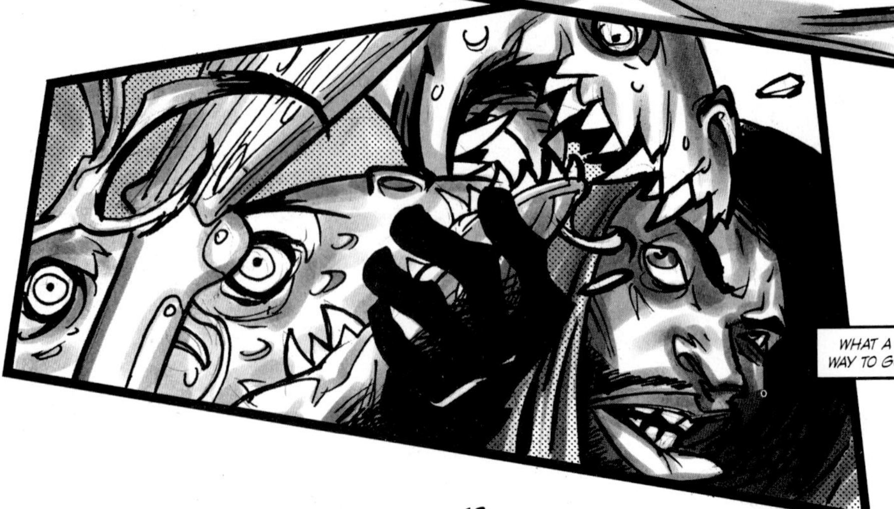
WHAT A WAY TO GO.

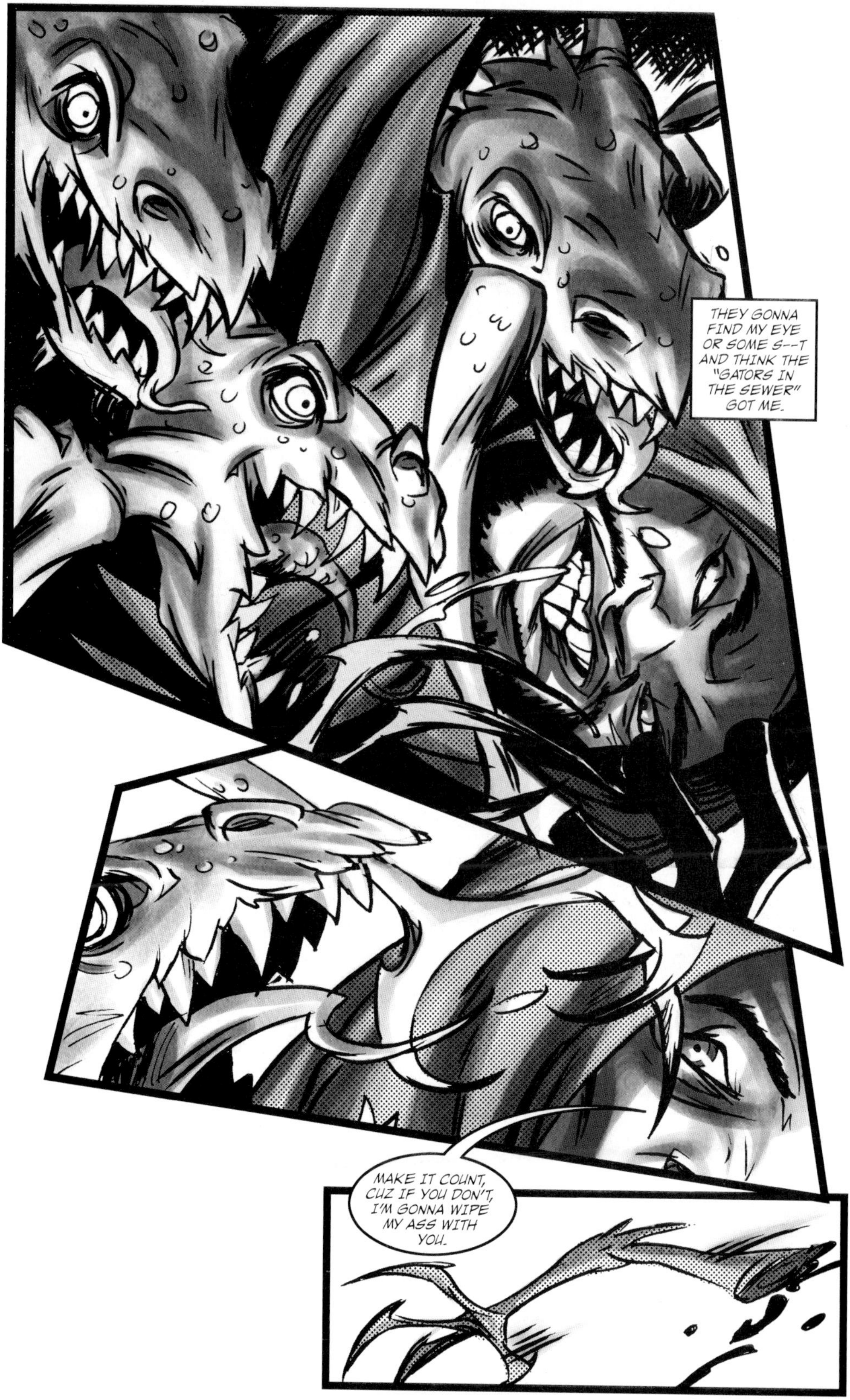
THEY GONNA FIND MY EYE OR SOME S--T AND THINK THE "GATORS IN THE SEWER" GOT ME.
MAKE IT COUNT, CUZ IF YOU DON'T, I'M GONNA WIPE MY ASS WITH YOU.

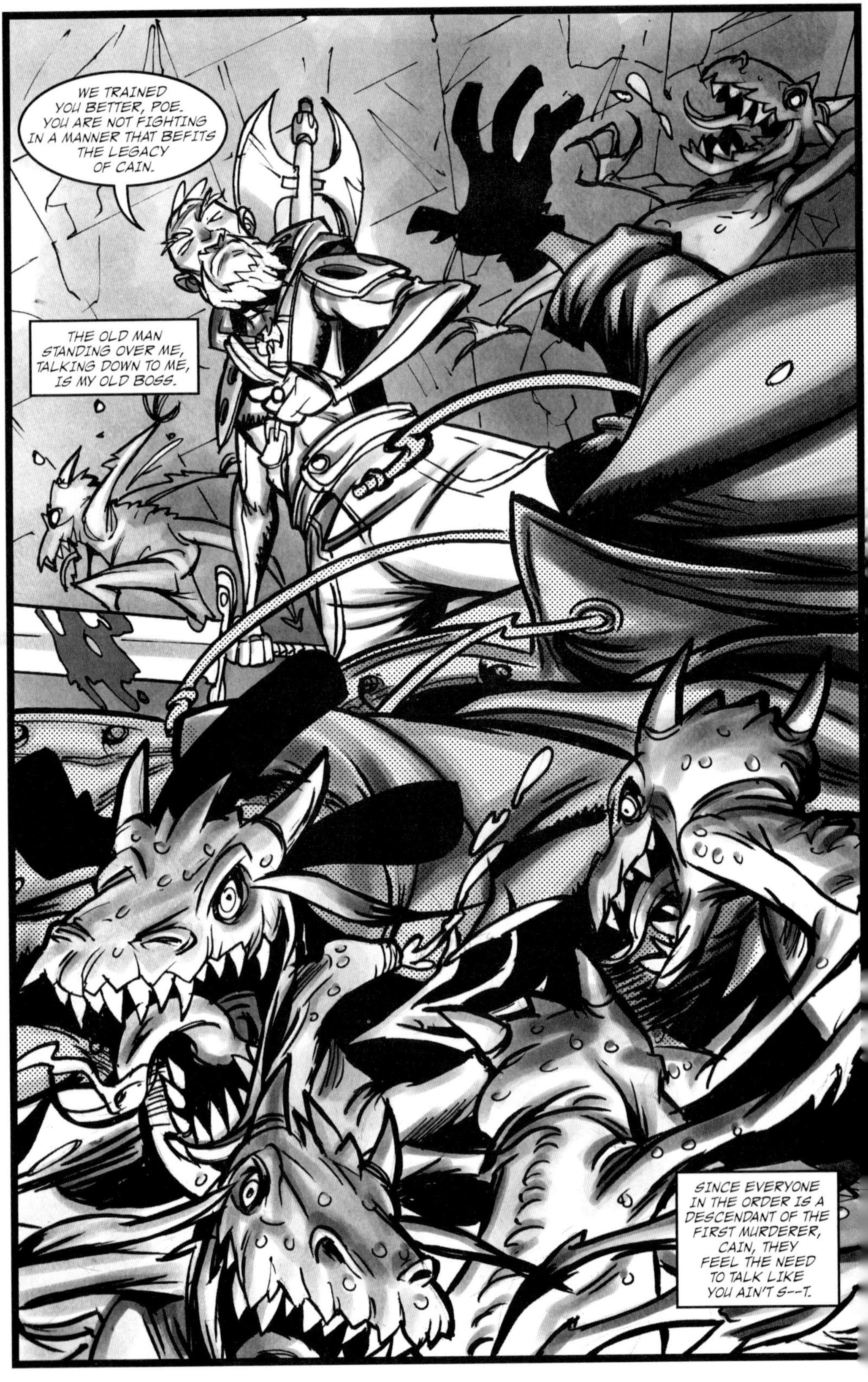
WE TRAINED YOU BETTER, POE. YOU ARE NOT FIGHTING IN A MANNER THAT BEFITS THE LEGACY OF CAIN.
THE OLD MAN STANDING OVER ME, TALKING DOWN TO ME, IS MY OLD BOSS.
SINCE EVERYONE IN THE ORDER IS A DESCENDANT OF THE FIRST MURDERER, CAIN, THEY FEEL THE NEED TO TALK LIKE YOU AIN'T S--T.

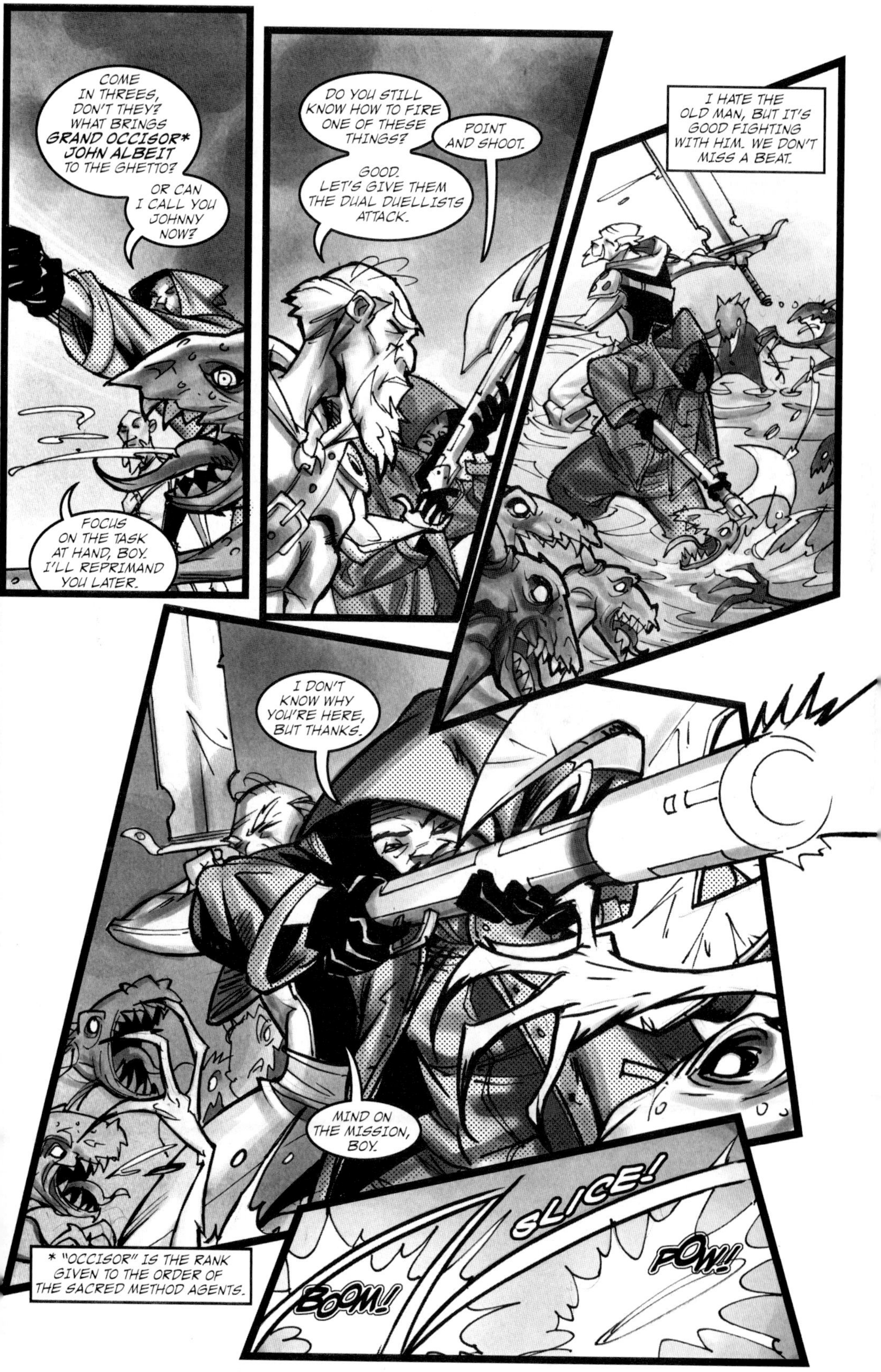
COME IN THREES, DON'T THEY? WHAT BRINGS GRAND OCCISOR* JOHN ALBEIT TO THE GHETTO?
OR CAN I CALL YOU JOHNNY NOW?
FOCUS ON THE TASK AT HAND, BOY. I'LL REPRIMAND YOU LATER.
DO YOU STILL KNOW HOW TO FIRE ONE OF THESE THINGS?
POINT AND SHOOT.
GOOD. LET'S GIVE THEM THE DUAL DUELLISTS ATTACK.
I HATE THE OLD MAN, BUT IT'S GOOD FIGHTING WITH HIM. WE DON'T MISS A BEAT.
I DON'T KNOW WHY YOU'RE HERE, BUT THANKS.
MIND ON THE MISSION, BOY.
SLICE!
POW!!
BOOM!
* "OCCISOR" IS THE RANK GIVEN TO THE ORDER OF THE SACRED METHOD AGENTS.

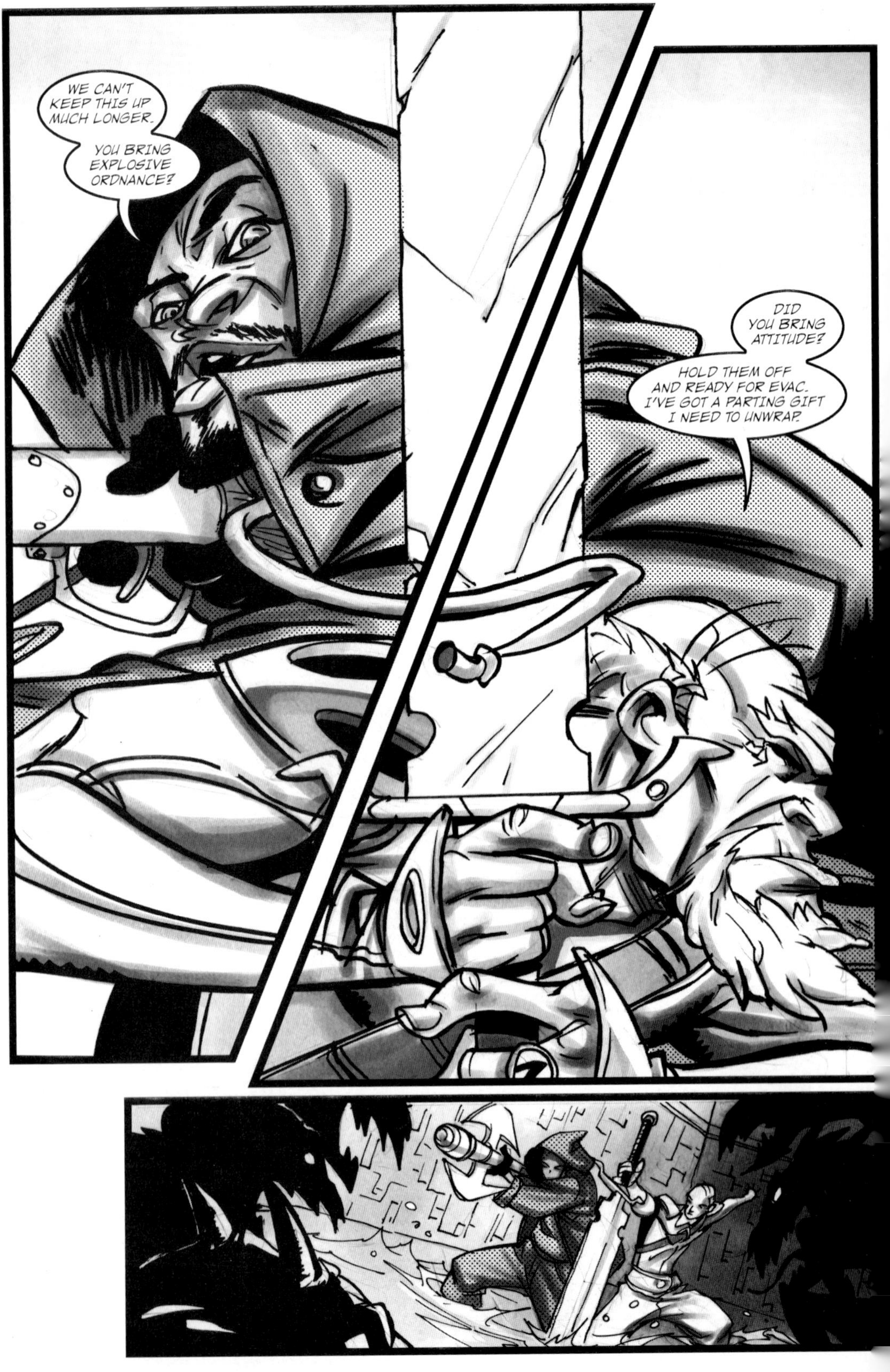

WE CAN'T KEEP THIS UP MUCH LONGER.
YOU BRING EXPLOSIVE ORDNANCE?
DID YOU BRING ATTITUDE?
HOLD THEM OFF AND READY FOR EVAC. I'VE GOT A PARTING GIFT I NEED TO UNWRAP.

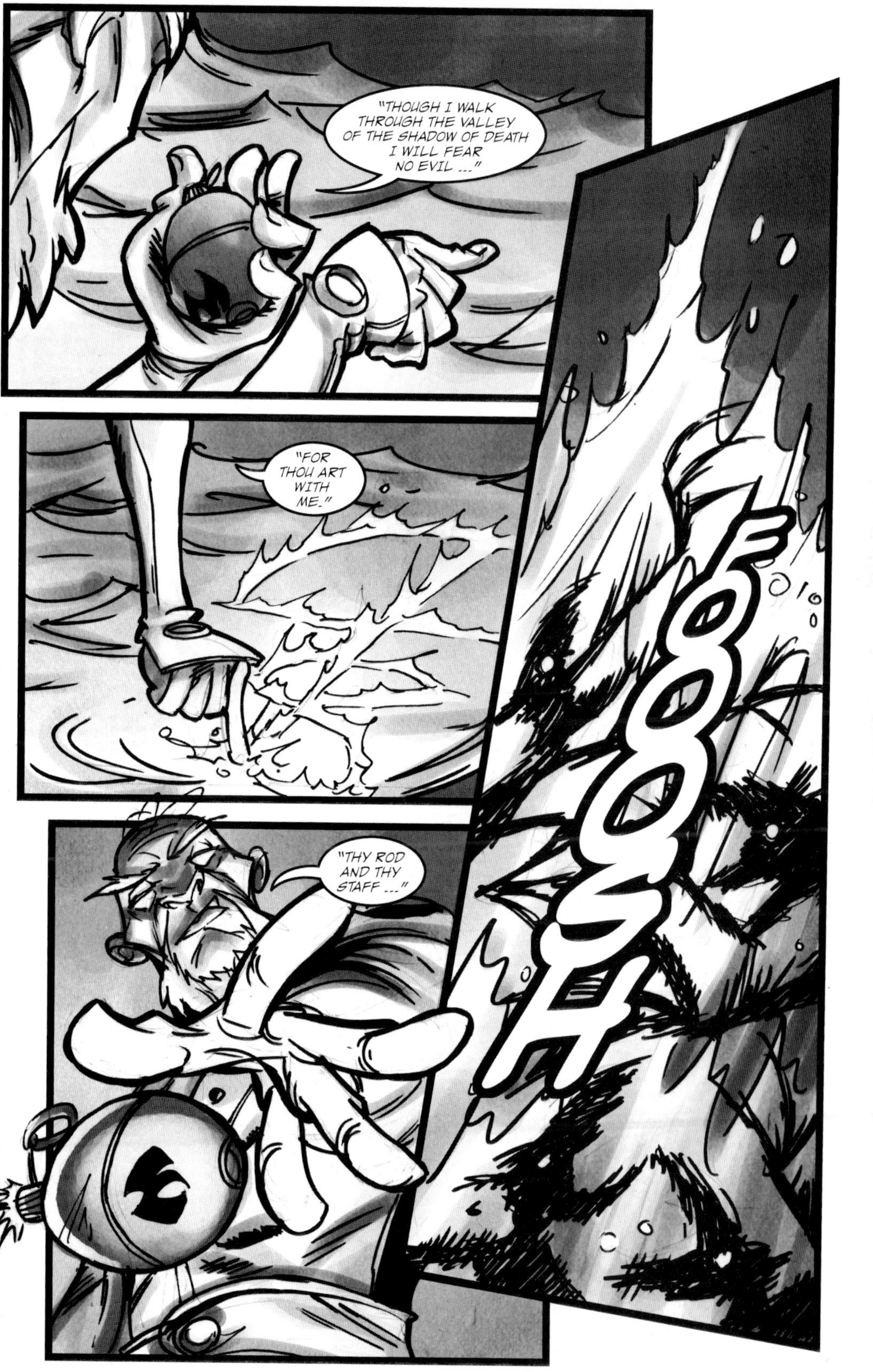
"THOUGH I WALK THROUGH THE VALLEY OF THE SHADOW OF DEATH I WILL FEAR NO EVIL ..."
"FOR THOU ART WITH ME."
"THY ROD AND THY STAFF ..."
FOOOSH

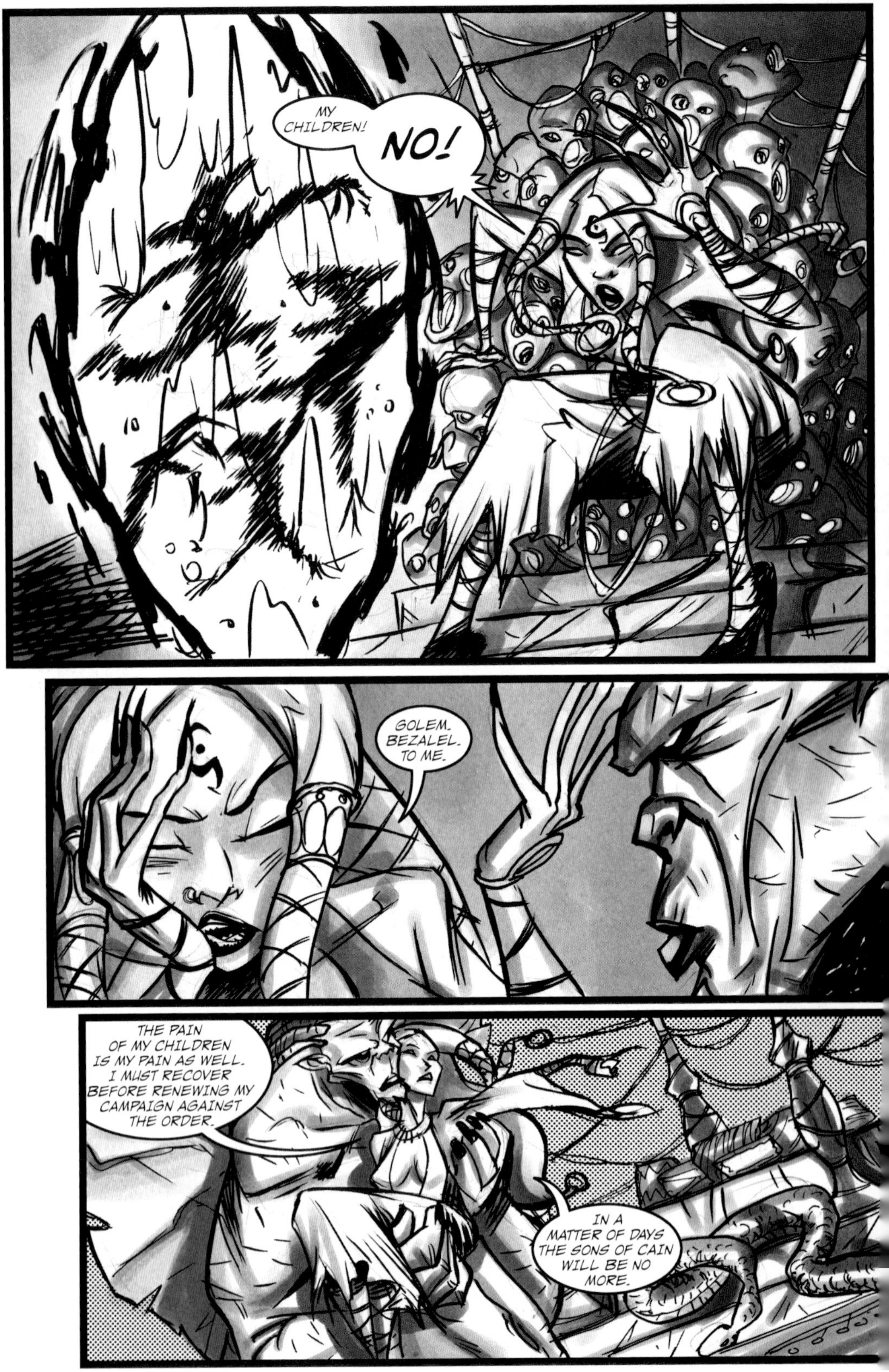
MY CHILDREN!
NO!
GOLEM. BEZALEL. TO ME.
THE PAIN OF MY CHILDREN IS MY PAIN AS WELL. I MUST RECOVER BEFORE RENEWING MY CAMPAIGN AGAINST THE ORDER.
IN A MATTER OF DAYS THE SONS OF CAIN WILL BE NO MORE.

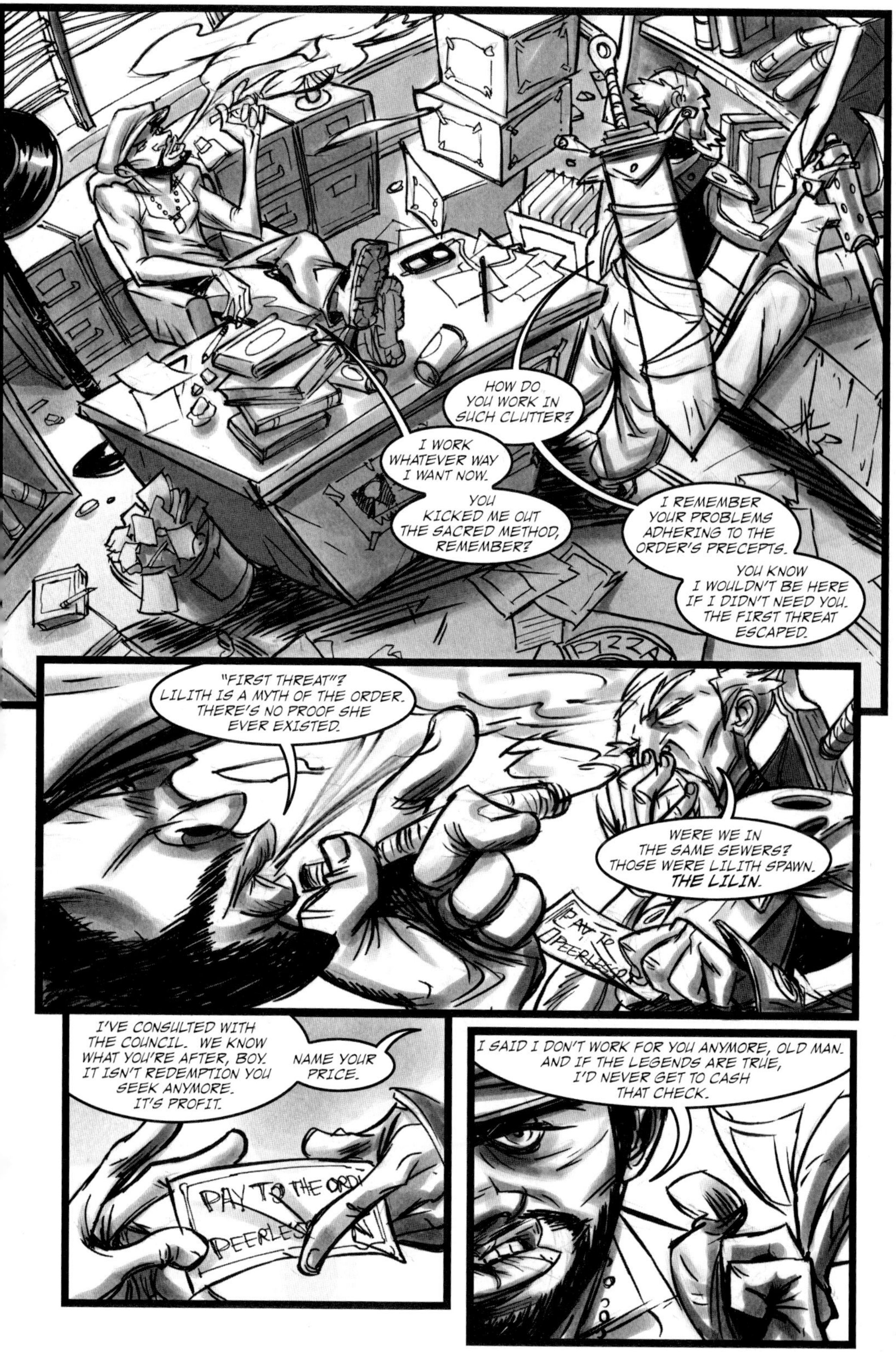
HOW DO YOU WORK IN SUCH CLUTTER?
I WORK WHATEVER WAY I WANT NOW.
YOU KICKED ME OUT THE SACRED METHOD, REMEMBER?
I REMEMBER YOUR PROBLEMS ADHERING TO THE ORDER'S PRECEPTS.
YOU KNOW I WOULDN'T BE HERE IF I DIDN'T NEED YOU. THE FIRST THREAT ESCAPED.
PIZZA
"FIRST THREAT"? LILITH IS A MYTH OF THE ORDER. THERE'S NO PROOF SHE EVER EXISTED.
WERE WE IN THE SAME SEWERS? THOSE WERE LILITH SPAWN. **THE LILIN.**
PAY TO
PEERLESS
I'VE CONSULTED WITH THE COUNCIL. WE KNOW WHAT YOU'RE AFTER, BOY. IT ISN'T REDEMPTION YOU SEEK ANYMORE. IT'S PROFIT.
NAME YOUR PRICE.
PAY TO THE ORD
PEERLES
I SAID I DON'T WORK FOR YOU ANYMORE, OLD MAN. AND IF THE LEGENDS ARE TRUE, I'D NEVER GET TO CASH THAT CHECK.

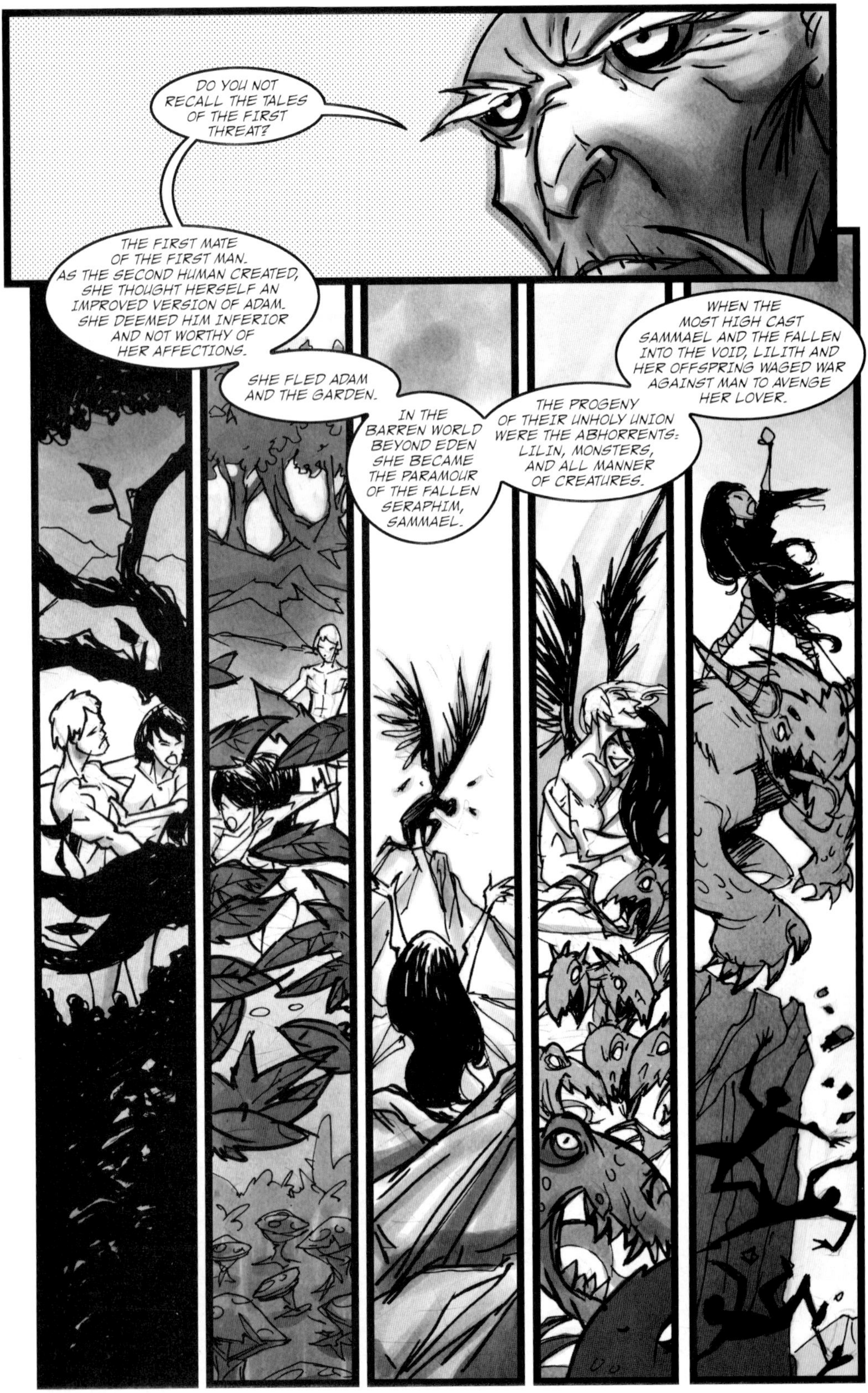
DO YOU NOT RECALL THE TALES OF THE FIRST THREAT?
THE FIRST MATE OF THE FIRST MAN. AS THE SECOND HUMAN CREATED, SHE THOUGHT HERSELF AN IMPROVED VERSION OF ADAM. SHE DEEMED HIM INFERIOR AND NOT WORTHY OF HER AFFECTIONS.
SHE FLED ADAM AND THE GARDEN.
IN THE BARREN WORLD BEYOND EDEN SHE BECAME THE PARAMOUR OF THE FALLEN SERAPHIM, SAMMAEL.
THE PROGENY OF THEIR UNHOLY UNION WERE THE ABHORRENTS: LILIN, MONSTERS, AND ALL MANNER OF CREATURES.
WHEN THE MOST HIGH CAST SAMMAEL AND THE FALLEN INTO THE VOID, LILITH AND HER OFFSPRING WAGED WAR AGAINST MAN TO AVENGE HER LOVER.

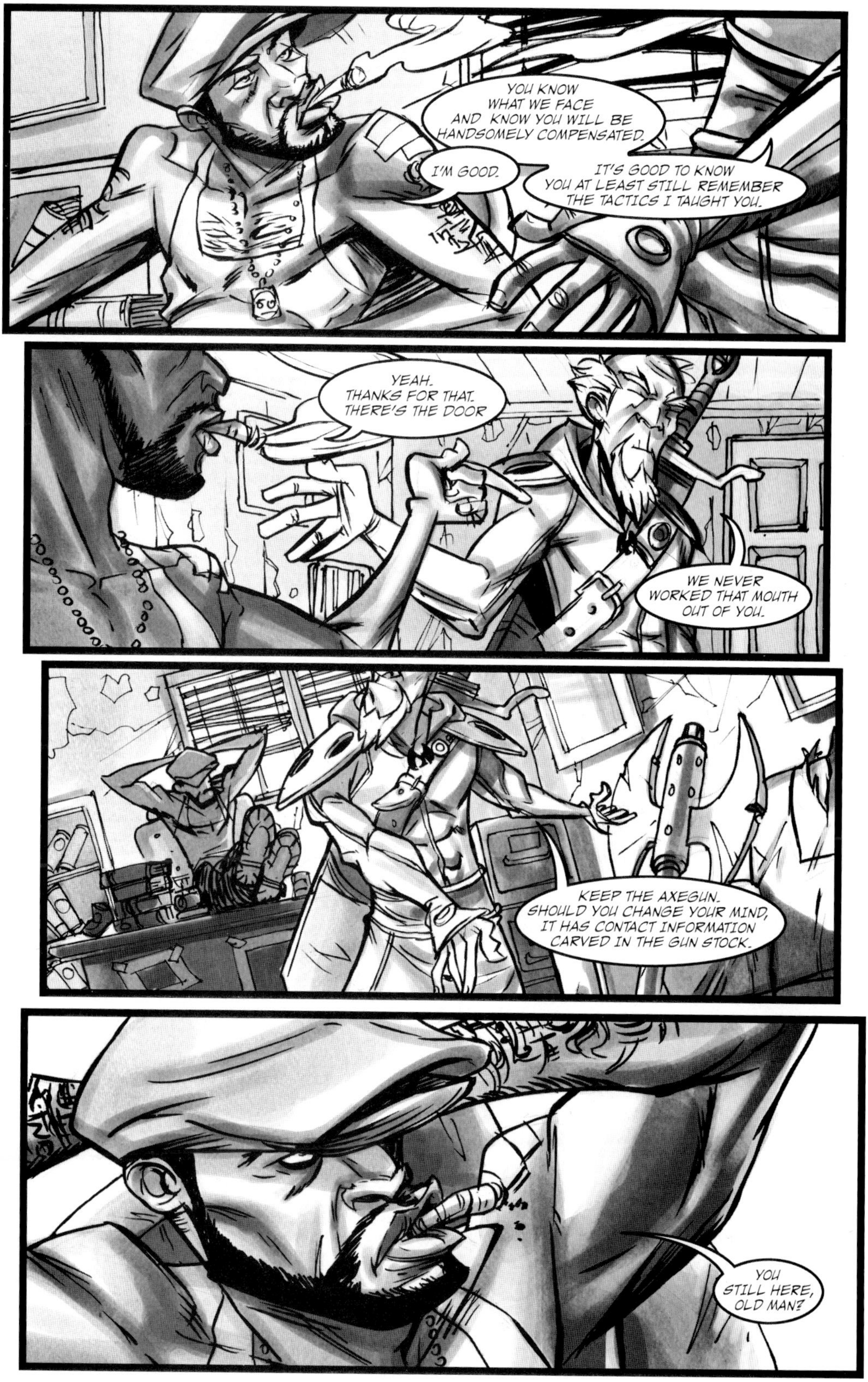
YOU KNOW WHAT WE FACE AND KNOW YOU WILL BE HANDSOMELY COMPENSATED.
I'M GOOD.
IT'S GOOD TO KNOW YOU AT LEAST STILL REMEMBER THE TACTICS I TAUGHT YOU.
YEAH. THANKS FOR THAT. THERE'S THE DOOR
WE NEVER WORKED THAT MOUTH OUT OF YOU.
KEEP THE AXEGUN. SHOULD YOU CHANGE YOUR MIND, IT HAS CONTACT INFORMATION CARVED IN THE GUN STOCK.
YOU STILL HERE, OLD MAN?

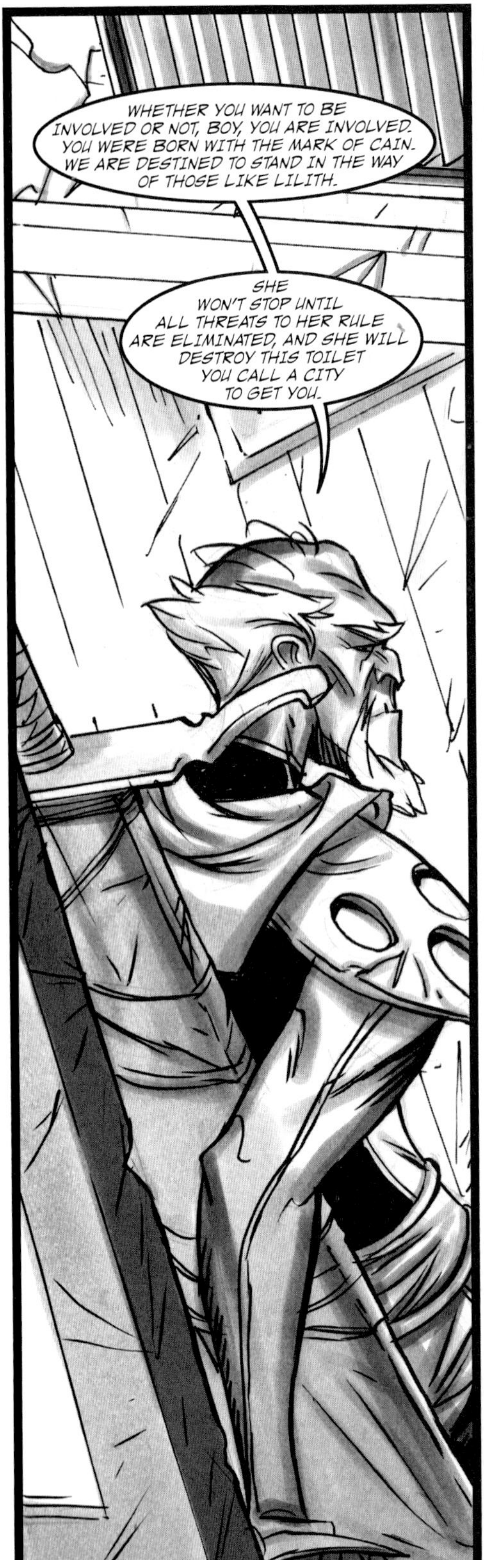
WHETHER YOU WANT TO BE INVOLVED OR NOT, BOY, YOU ARE INVOLVED. YOU WERE BORN WITH THE MARK OF CAIN. WE ARE DESTINED TO STAND IN THE WAY OF THOSE LIKE LILITH.
SHE WON'T STOP UNTIL ALL THREATS TO HER RULE ARE ELIMINATED, AND SHE WILL DESTROY THIS TOILET YOU CALL A CITY TO GET YOU.

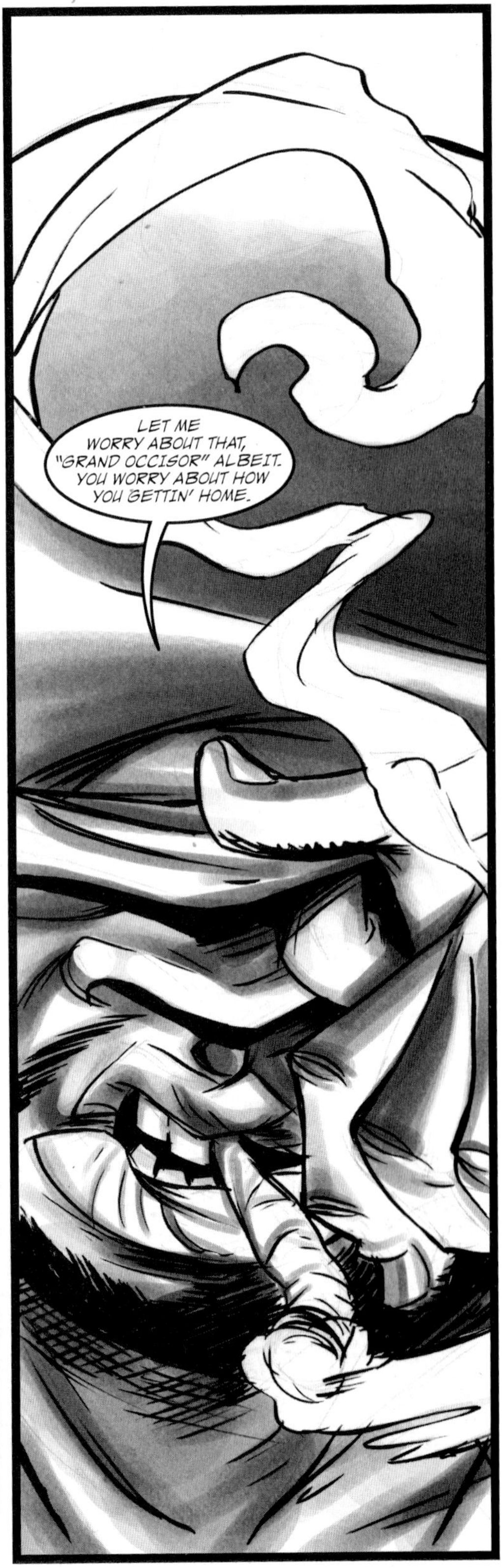
LET ME WORRY ABOUT THAT, "GRAND OCCISOR" ALBEIT. YOU WORRY ABOUT HOW YOU GETTIN' HOME.

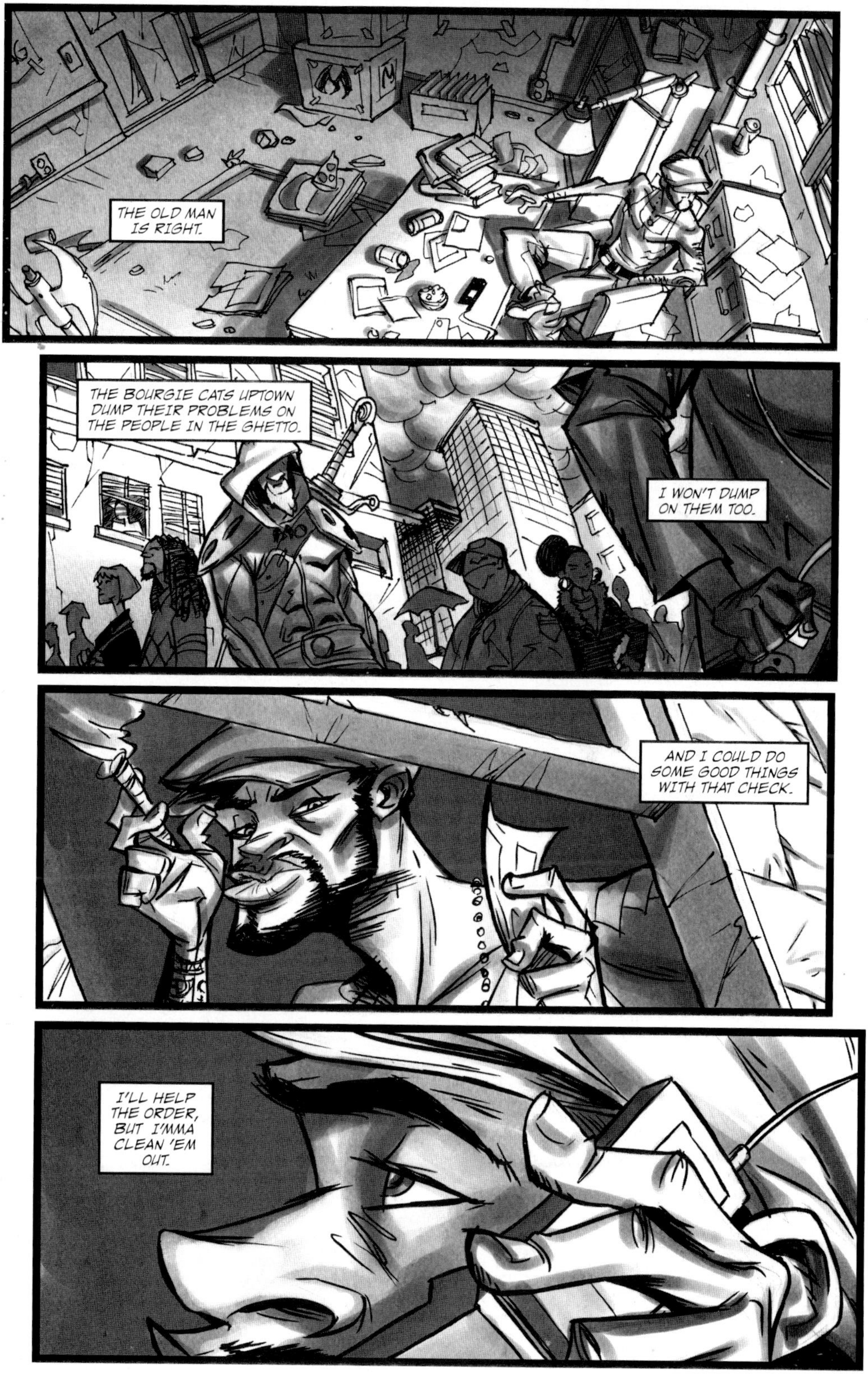
THE OLD MAN IS RIGHT.
THE BOURGIE CATS UPTOWN DUMP THEIR PROBLEMS ON THE PEOPLE IN THE GHETTO.
I WON'T DUMP ON THEM TOO.
AND I COULD DO SOME GOOD THINGS WITH THAT CHECK.
I'LL HELP THE ORDER, BUT I'MMA CLEAN 'EM OUT.

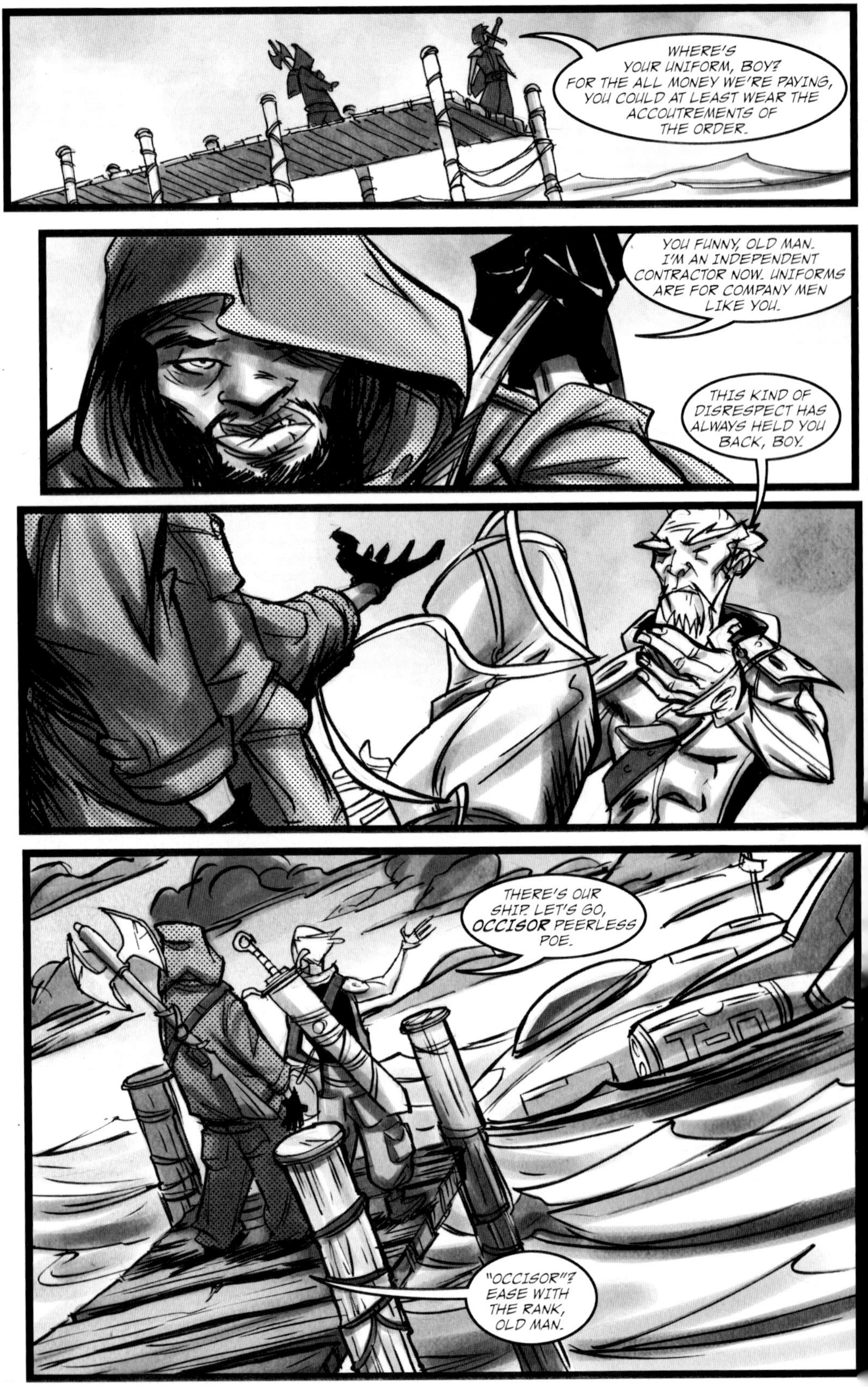
WHERE'S YOUR UNIFORM, BOY? FOR THE ALL MONEY WE'RE PAYING, YOU COULD AT LEAST WEAR THE ACCOUTREMENTS OF THE ORDER.
YOU FUNNY, OLD MAN. I'M AN INDEPENDENT CONTRACTOR NOW. UNIFORMS ARE FOR COMPANY MEN LIKE YOU.
THIS KIND OF DISRESPECT HAS ALWAYS HELD YOU BACK, BOY.
THERE'S OUR SHIP. LET'S GO, OCCISOR PEERLESS POE.
"OCCISOR"? EASE WITH THE RANK, OLD MAN.

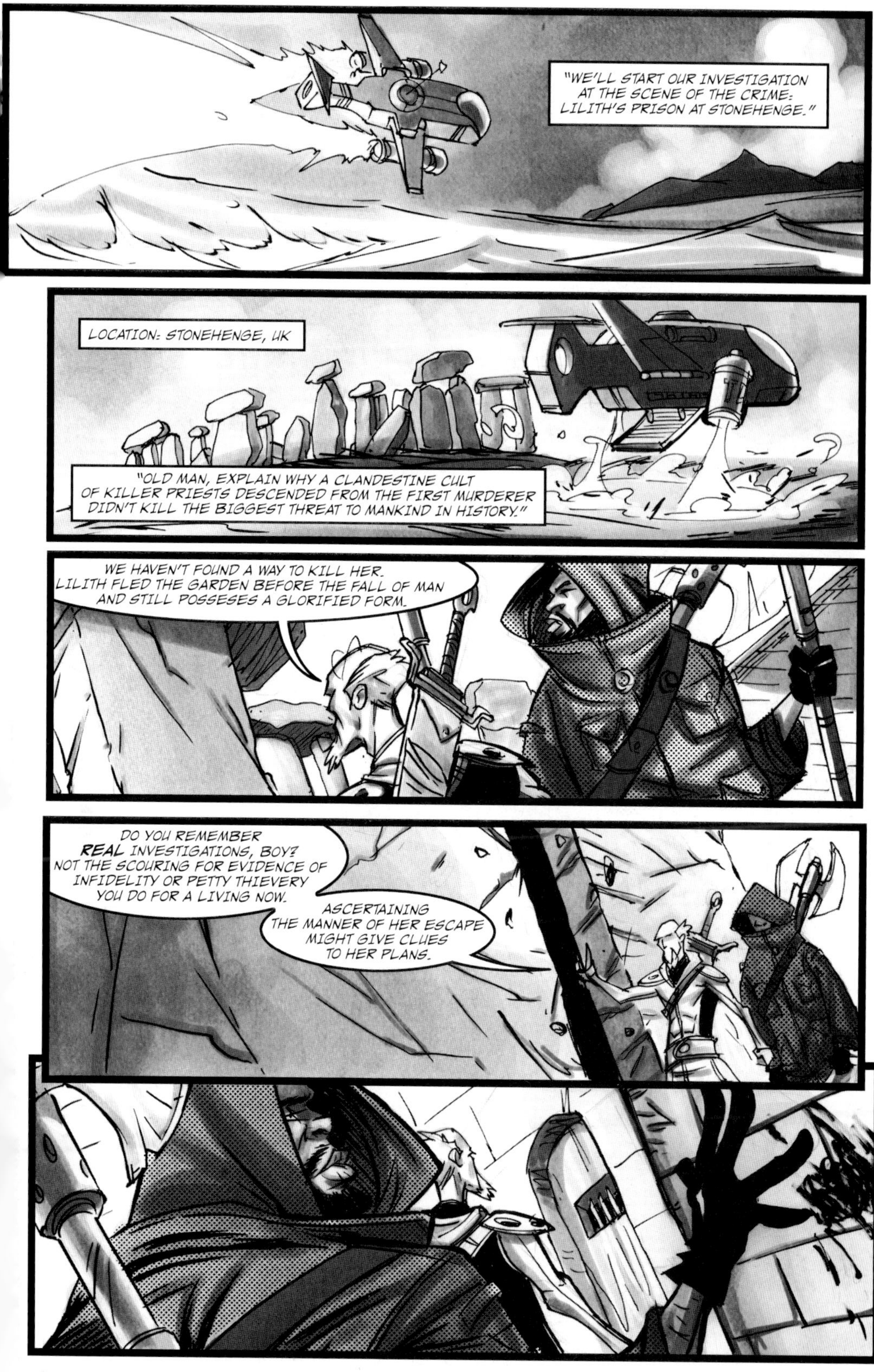
"WE'LL START OUR INVESTIGATION AT THE SCENE OF THE CRIME: LILITH'S PRISON AT STONEHENGE."
LOCATION: STONEHENGE, UK
"OLD MAN, EXPLAIN WHY A CLANDESTINE CULT OF KILLER PRIESTS DESCENDED FROM THE FIRST MURDERER DIDN'T KILL THE BIGGEST THREAT TO MANKIND IN HISTORY."
WE HAVEN'T FOUND A WAY TO KILL HER. LILITH FLED THE GARDEN BEFORE THE FALL OF MAN AND STILL POSSESES A GLORIFIED FORM.
DO YOU REMEMBER **REAL** INVESTIGATIONS, BOY? NOT THE SCOURING FOR EVIDENCE OF INFIDELITY OR PETTY THIEVERY YOU DO FOR A LIVING NOW.
ASCERTAINING THE MANNER OF HER ESCAPE MIGHT GIVE CLUES TO HER PLANS.

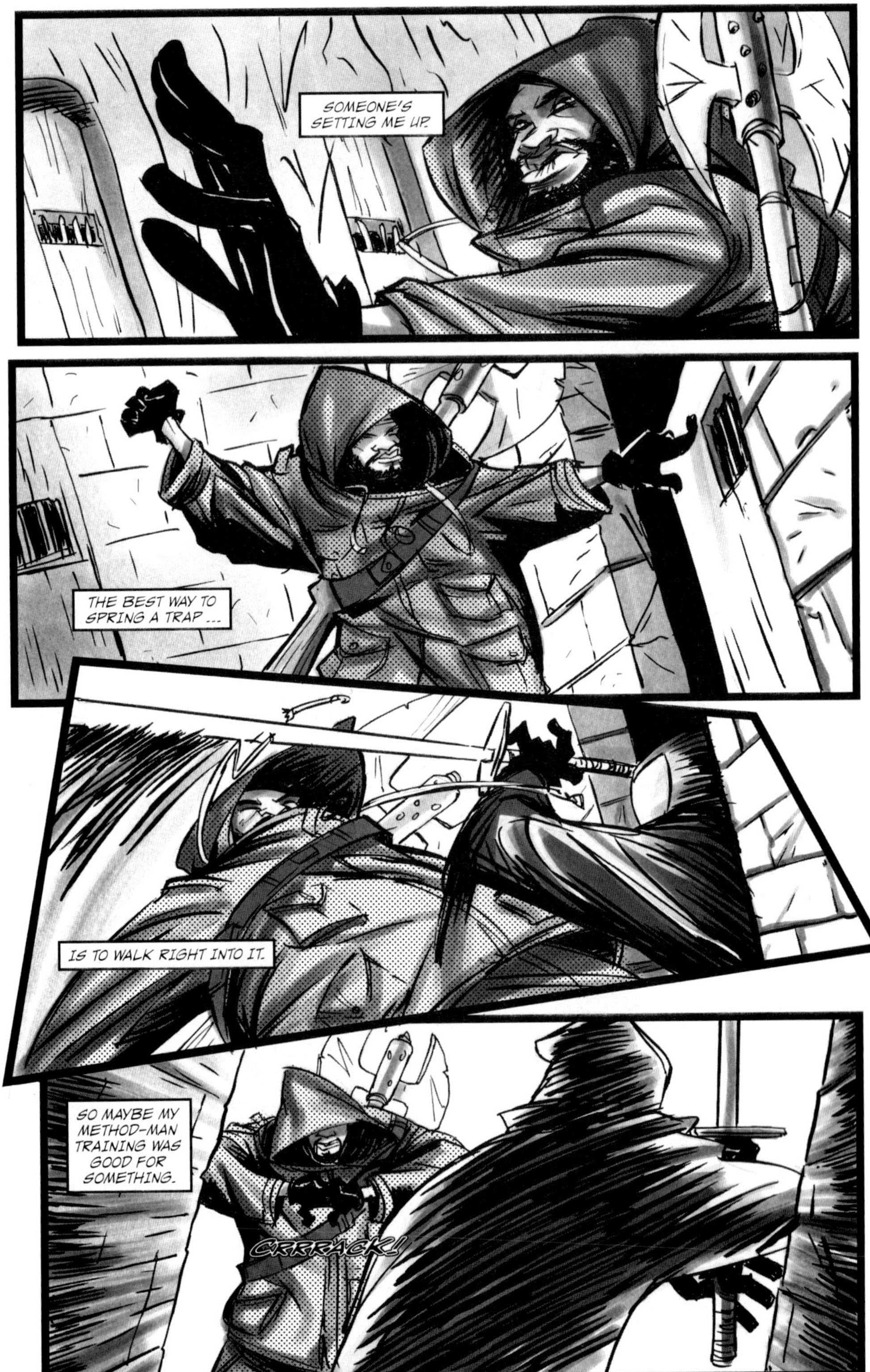
SOMEONE'S SETTING ME UP.
THE BEST WAY TO SPRING A TRAP ...
IS TO WALK RIGHT INTO IT.
SO MAYBE MY METHOD-MAN TRAINING WAS GOOD FOR SOMETHING.
CRRRACK!

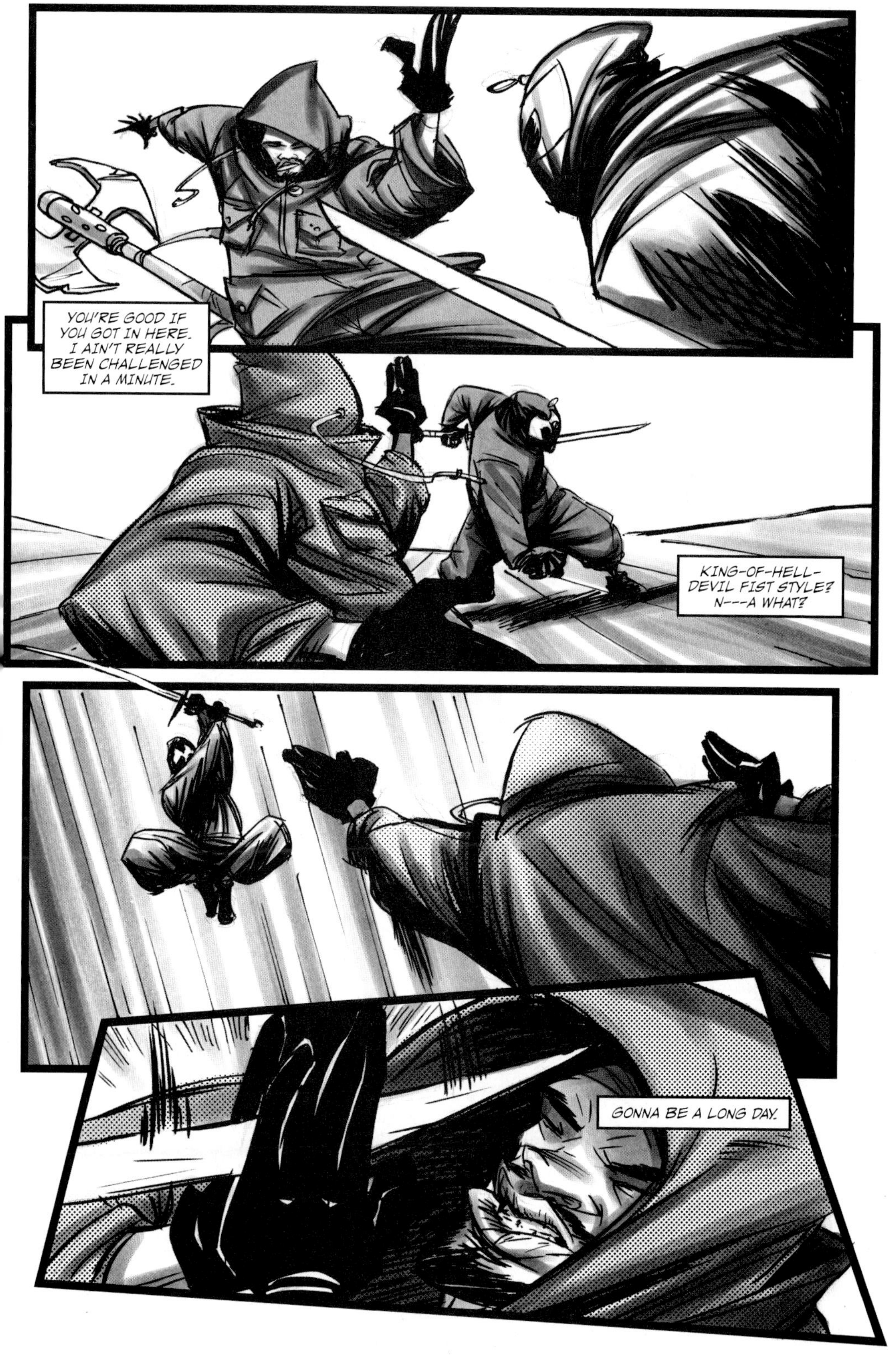
YOU'RE GOOD IF YOU GOT IN HERE. I AIN'T REALLY BEEN CHALLENGED IN A MINUTE.
KING-OF-HELL-DEVIL FIST STYLE? N---A WHAT?
GONNA BE A LONG DAY.

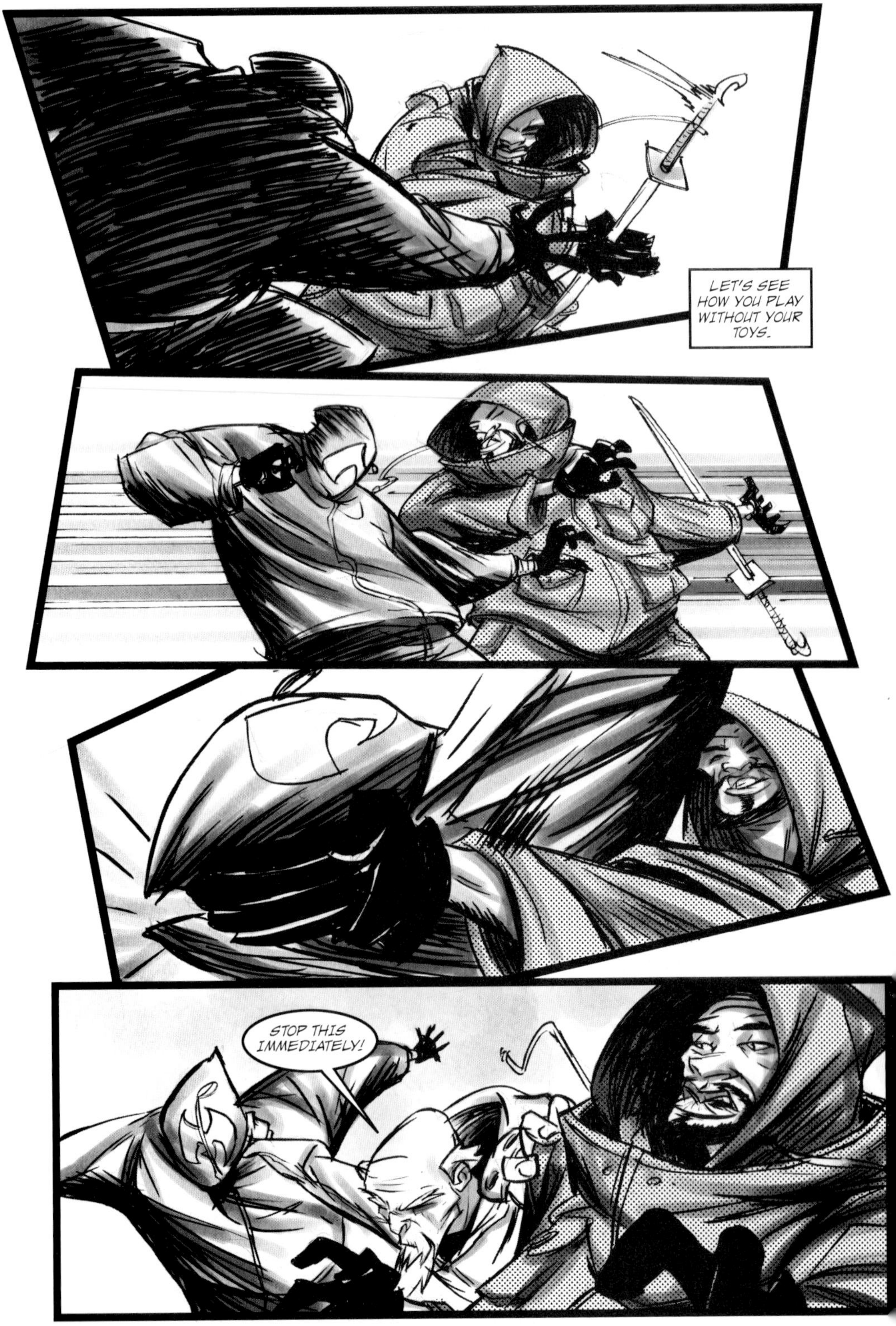
LET'S SEE HOW YOU PLAY WITHOUT YOUR TOYS.
STOP THIS IMMEDIATELY!

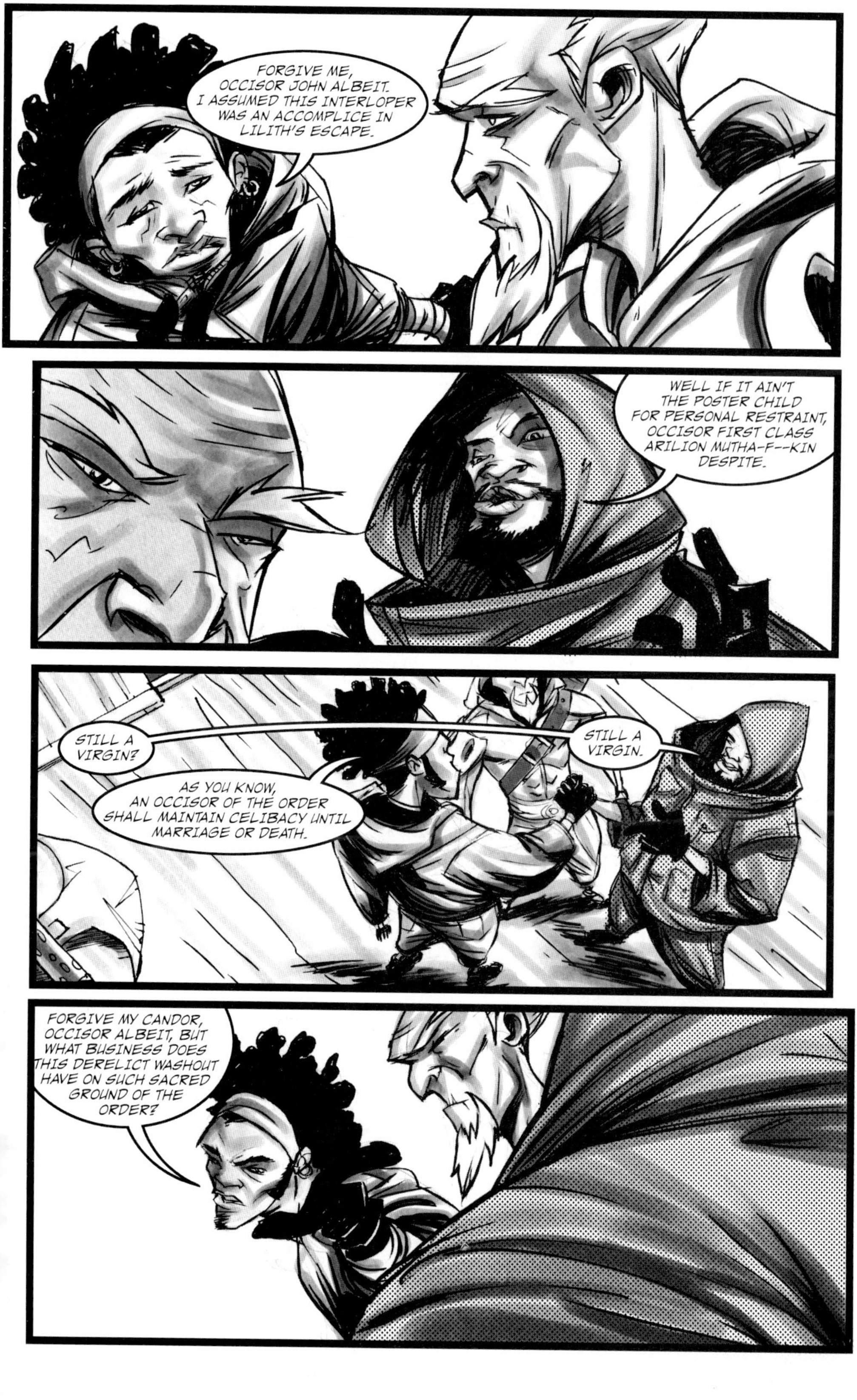
FORGIVE ME, OCCISOR JOHN ALBEIT. I ASSUMED THIS INTERLOPER WAS AN ACCOMPLICE IN LILITH'S ESCAPE.
WELL IF IT AIN'T THE POSTER CHILD FOR PERSONAL RESTRAINT, OCCISOR FIRST CLASS ARILION MUTHA-F--KIN DESPITE.
STILL A VIRGIN?
AS YOU KNOW, AN OCCISOR OF THE ORDER SHALL MAINTAIN CELIBACY UNTIL MARRIAGE OR DEATH.
STILL A VIRGIN.
FORGIVE MY CANDOR, OCCISOR ALBEIT, BUT WHAT BUSINESS DOES THIS DERELICT WASHOUT HAVE ON SUCH SACRED GROUND OF THE ORDER?

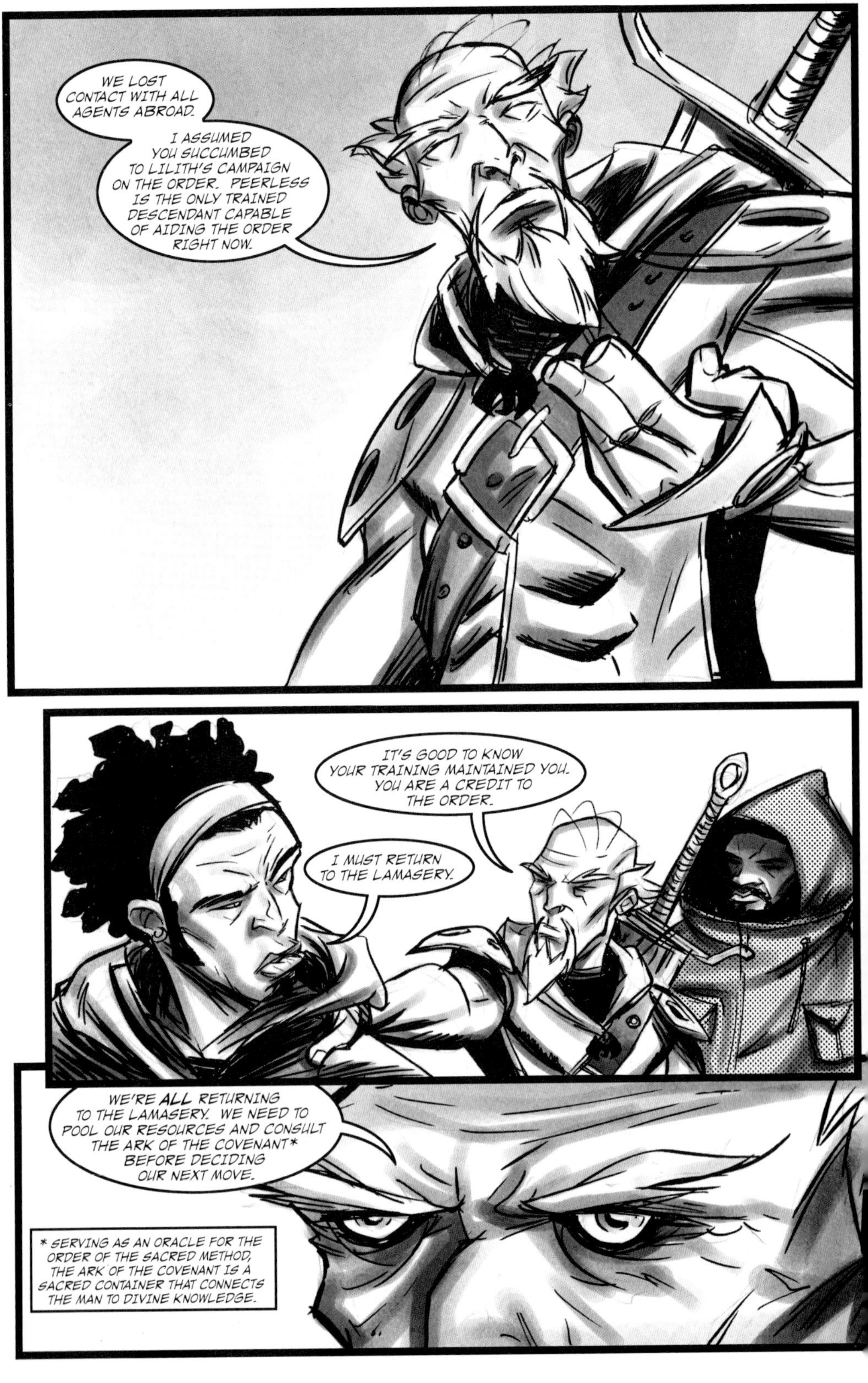
WE LOST CONTACT WITH ALL AGENTS ABROAD.
I ASSUMED YOU SUCCUMBED TO LILITH'S CAMPAIGN ON THE ORDER. PEERLESS IS THE ONLY TRAINED DESCENDANT CAPABLE OF AIDING THE ORDER RIGHT NOW.
IT'S GOOD TO KNOW YOUR TRAINING MAINTAINED YOU. YOU ARE A CREDIT TO THE ORDER.
I MUST RETURN TO THE LAMASERY.
WE'RE ALL RETURNING TO THE LAMASERY. WE NEED TO POOL OUR RESOURCES AND CONSULT THE ARK OF THE COVENANT* BEFORE DECIDING OUR NEXT MOVE.
* SERVING AS AN ORACLE FOR THE ORDER OF THE SACRED METHOD, THE ARK OF THE COVENANT IS A SACRED CONTAINER THAT CONNECTS THE MAN TO DIVINE KNOWLEDGE.

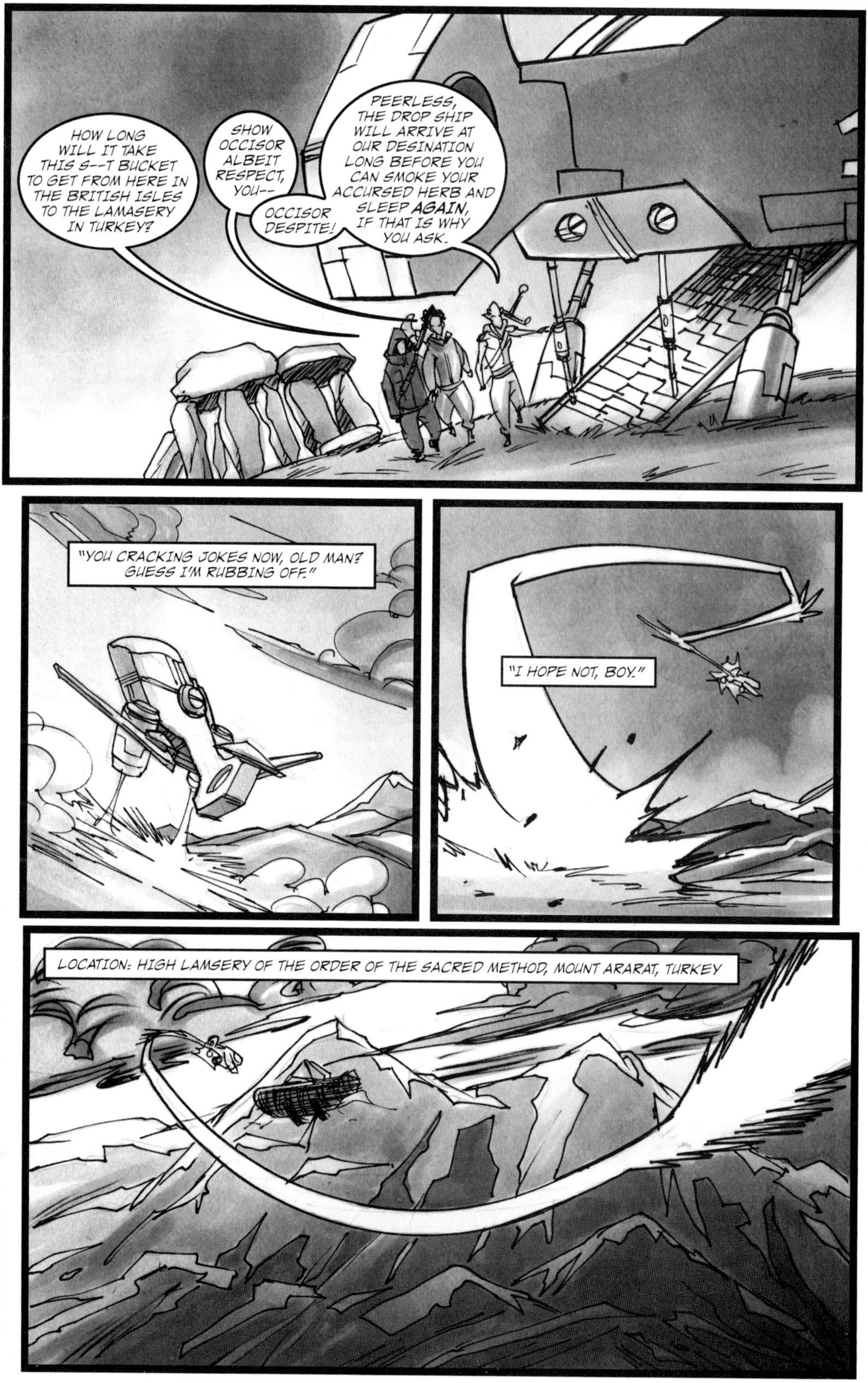
HOW LONG WILL IT TAKE THIS S--T BUCKET TO GET FROM HERE IN THE BRITISH ISLES TO THE LAMASERY IN TURKEY?
SHOW OCCISOR ALBEIT RESPECT, YOU--
OCCISOR DESPITE!
PEERLESS, THE DROP SHIP WILL ARRIVE AT OUR DESINATION LONG BEFORE YOU CAN SMOKE YOUR ACCURSED HERB AND SLEEP AGAIN, IF THAT IS WHY YOU ASK.
"YOU CRACKING JOKES NOW, OLD MAN? GUESS I'M RUBBING OFF."
"I HOPE NOT, BOY."
LOCATION: HIGH LAMSERY OF THE ORDER OF THE SACRED METHOD, MOUNT ARARAT, TURKEY

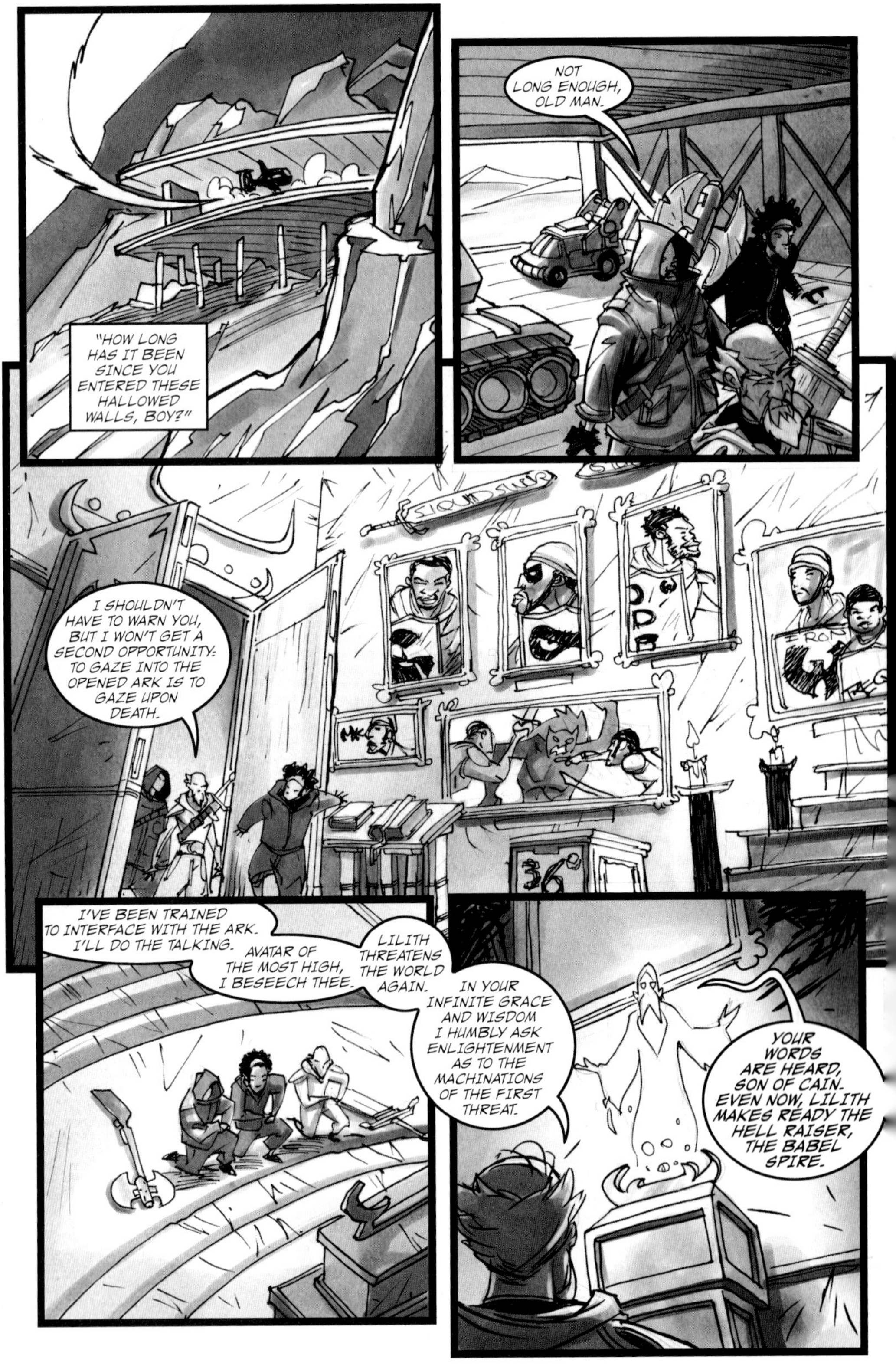
"HOW LONG HAS IT BEEN SINCE YOU ENTERED THESE HALLOWED WALLS, BOY?"
NOT LONG ENOUGH, OLD MAN.
I SHOULDN'T HAVE TO WARN YOU, BUT I WON'T GET A SECOND OPPORTUNITY: TO GAZE INTO THE OPENED ARK IS TO GAZE UPON DEATH.
I'VE BEEN TRAINED TO INTERFACE WITH THE ARK. I'LL DO THE TALKING.
AVATAR OF THE MOST HIGH, I BESEECH THEE.
LILITH THREATENS THE WORLD AGAIN.
IN YOUR INFINITE GRACE AND WISDOM I HUMBLY ASK ENLIGHTENMENT AS TO THE MACHINATIONS OF THE FIRST THREAT.
YOUR WORDS ARE HEARD, SON OF CAIN. EVEN NOW, LILITH MAKES READY THE HELL RAISER, THE BABEL SPIRE.

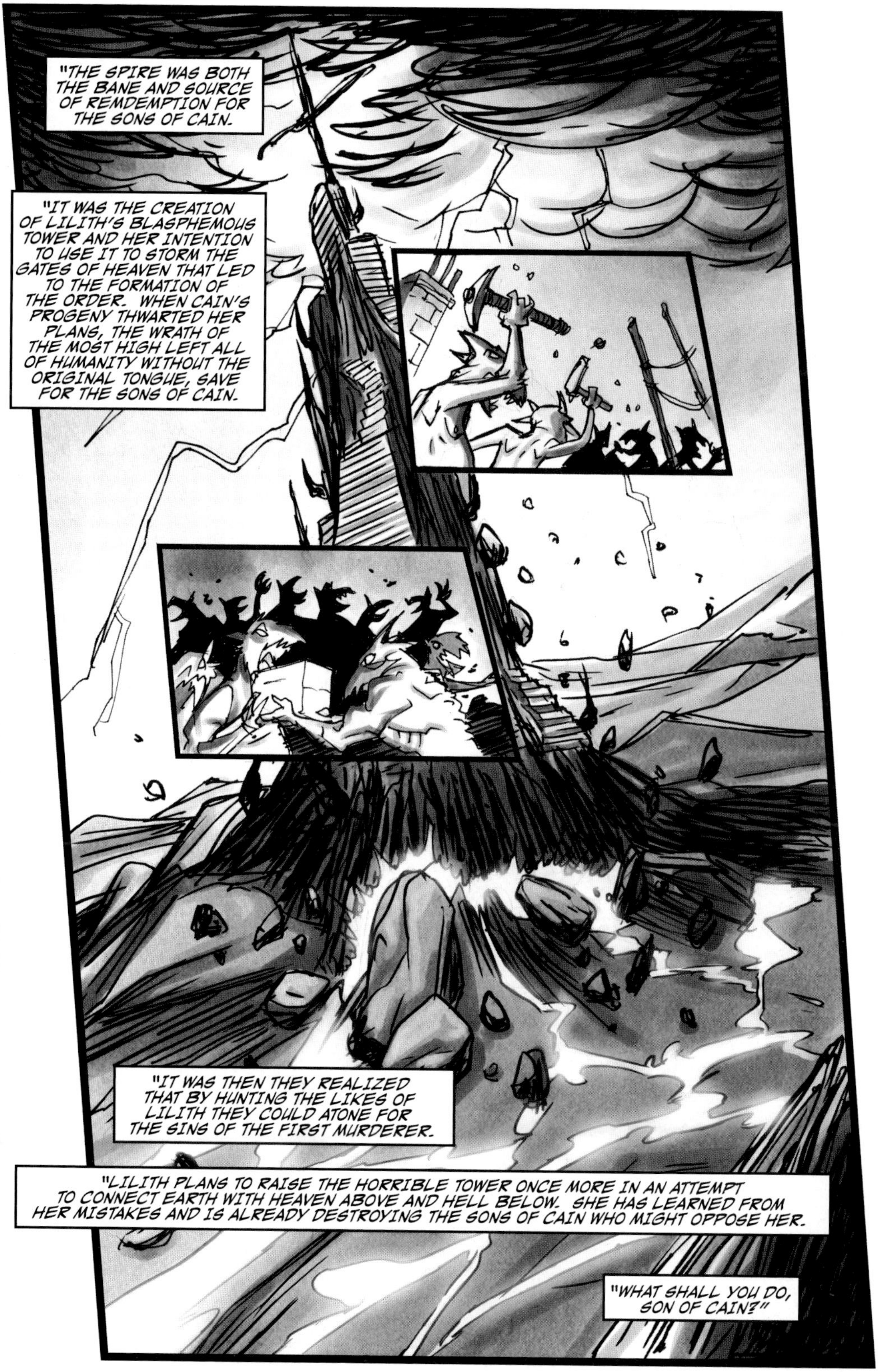
"THE SPIRE WAS BOTH THE BANE AND SOURCE OF REMDEMPTION FOR THE SONS OF CAIN.
"IT WAS THE CREATION OF LILITH'S BLASPHEMOUS TOWER AND HER INTENTION TO USE IT TO STORM THE GATES OF HEAVEN THAT LED TO THE FORMATION OF THE ORDER. WHEN CAIN'S PROGENY THWARTED HER PLANS, THE WRATH OF THE MOST HIGH LEFT ALL OF HUMANITY WITHOUT THE ORIGINAL TONGUE, SAVE FOR THE SONS OF CAIN.
"IT WAS THEN THEY REALIZED THAT BY HUNTING THE LIKES OF LILITH THEY COULD ATONE FOR THE SINS OF THE FIRST MURDERER.
"LILITH PLANS TO RAISE THE HORRIBLE TOWER ONCE MORE IN AN ATTEMPT TO CONNECT EARTH WITH HEAVEN ABOVE AND HELL BELOW. SHE HAS LEARNED FROM HER MISTAKES AND IS ALREADY DESTROYING THE SONS OF CAIN WHO MIGHT OPPOSE HER.
"WHAT SHALL YOU DO, SON OF CAIN?"

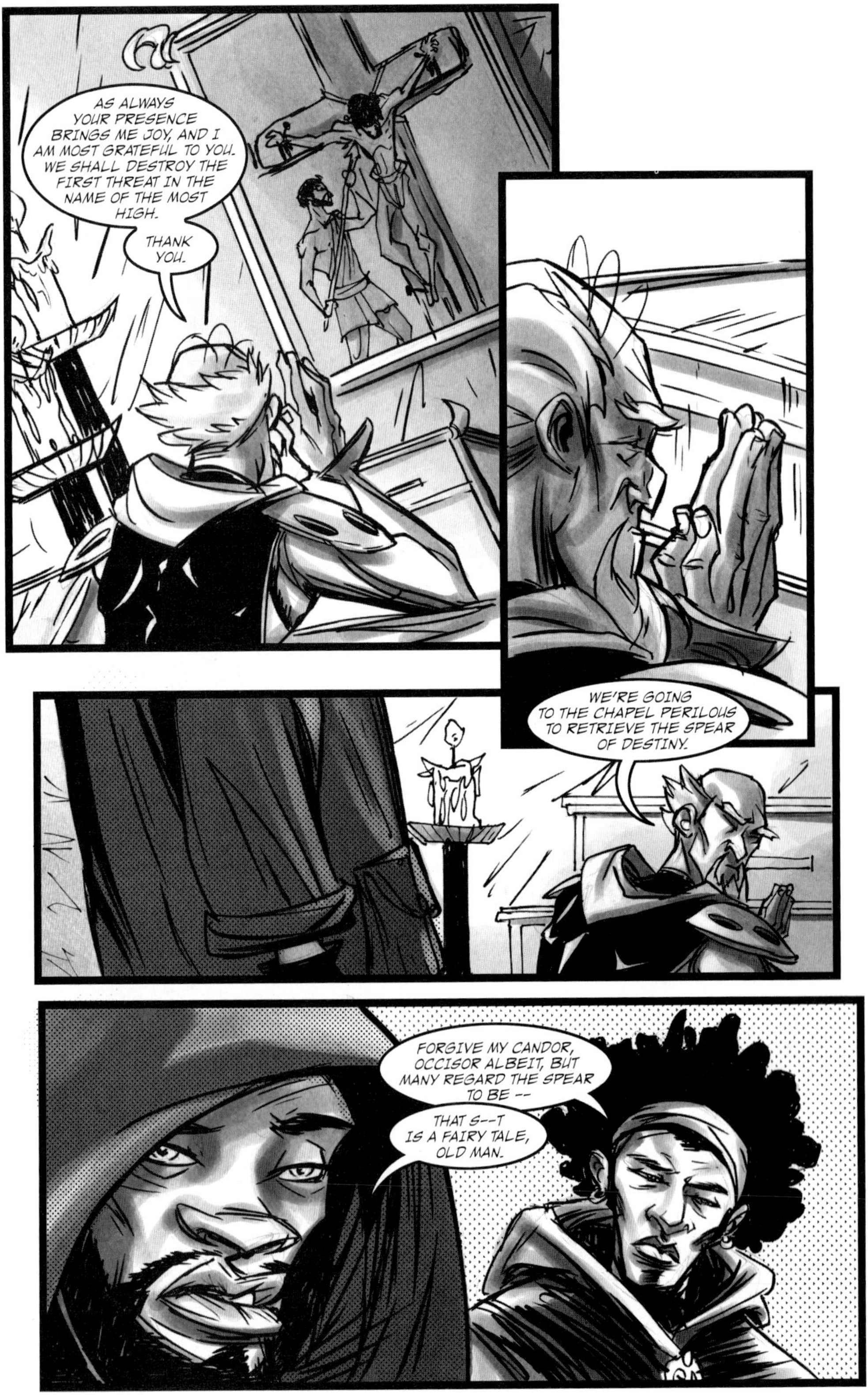
AS ALWAYS YOUR PRESENCE BRINGS ME JOY, AND I AM MOST GRATEFUL TO YOU. WE SHALL DESTROY THE FIRST THREAT IN THE NAME OF THE MOST HIGH.
THANK YOU.
WE'RE GOING TO THE CHAPEL PERILOUS TO RETRIEVE THE SPEAR OF DESTINY.
FORGIVE MY CANDOR, OCCISOR ALBEIT, BUT MANY REGARD THE SPEAR TO BE --
THAT S--T IS A FAIRY TALE, OLD MAN.

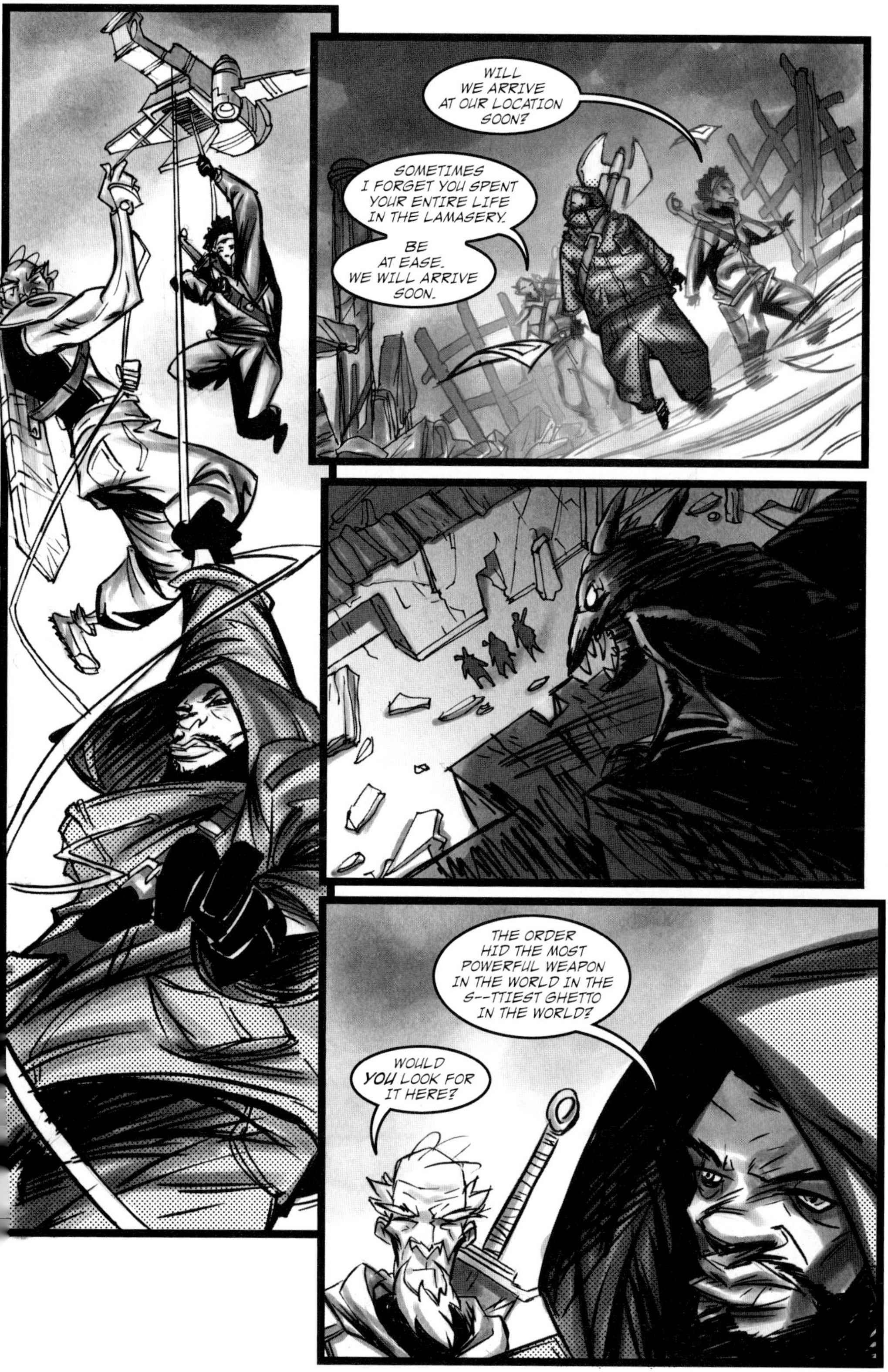
WILL WE ARRIVE AT OUR LOCATION SOON?
SOMETIMES I FORGET YOU SPENT YOUR ENTIRE LIFE IN THE LAMASERY.
BE AT EASE. WE WILL ARRIVE SOON.
THE ORDER HID THE MOST POWERFUL WEAPON IN THE WORLD IN THE S--TTIEST GHETTO IN THE WORLD?
WOULD YOU LOOK FOR IT HERE?

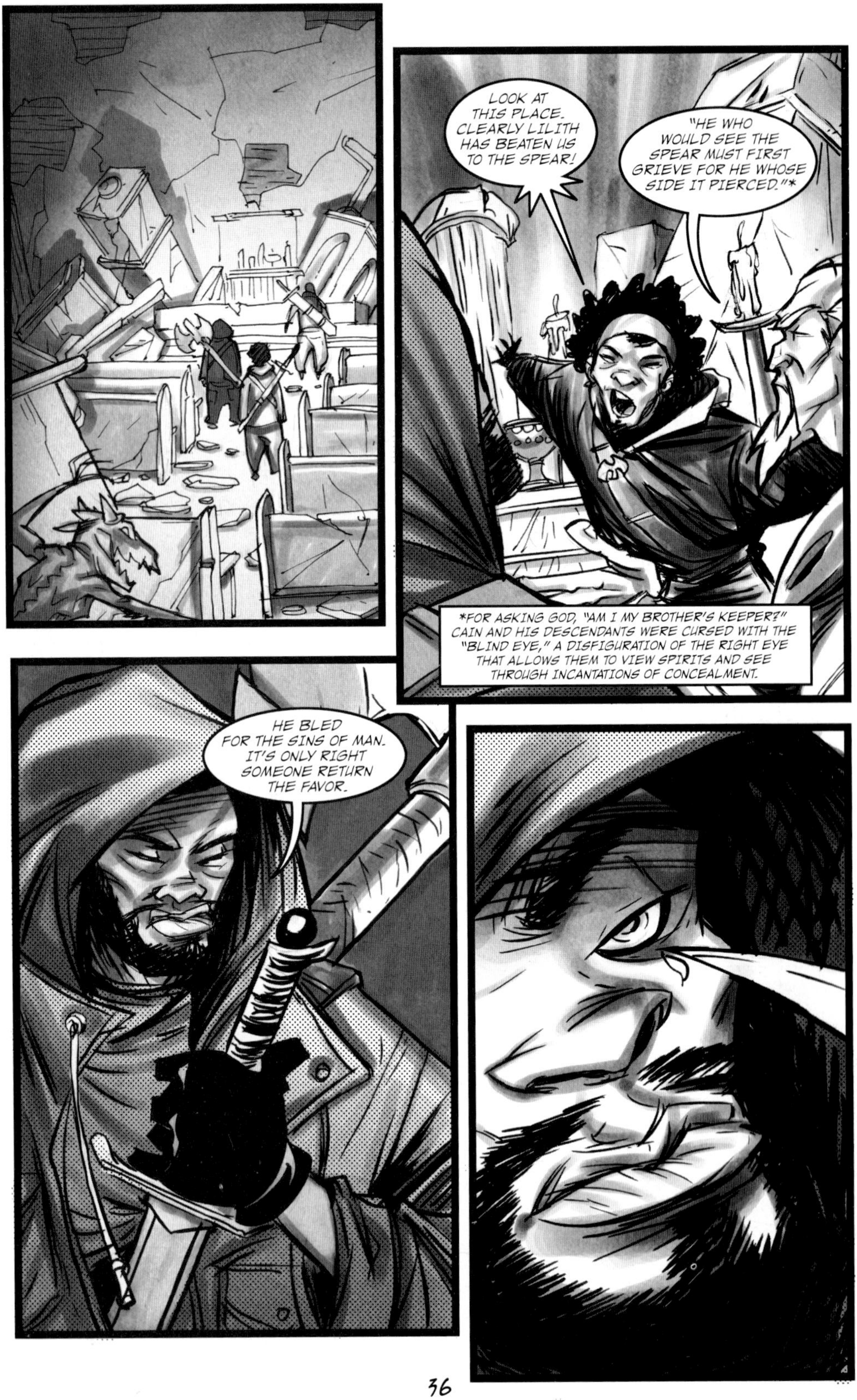
LOOK AT THIS PLACE. CLEARLY LILITH HAS BEATEN US TO THE SPEAR!
"HE WHO WOULD SEE THE SPEAR MUST FIRST GRIEVE FOR HE WHOSE SIDE IT PIERCED."*
*FOR ASKING GOD, "AM I MY BROTHER'S KEEPER?" CAIN AND HIS DESCENDANTS WERE CURSED WITH THE "BLIND EYE," A DISFIGURATION OF THE RIGHT EYE THAT ALLOWS THEM TO VIEW SPIRITS AND SEE THROUGH INCANTATIONS OF CONCEALMENT.
HE BLED FOR THE SINS OF MAN. IT'S ONLY RIGHT SOMEONE RETURN THE FAVOR.

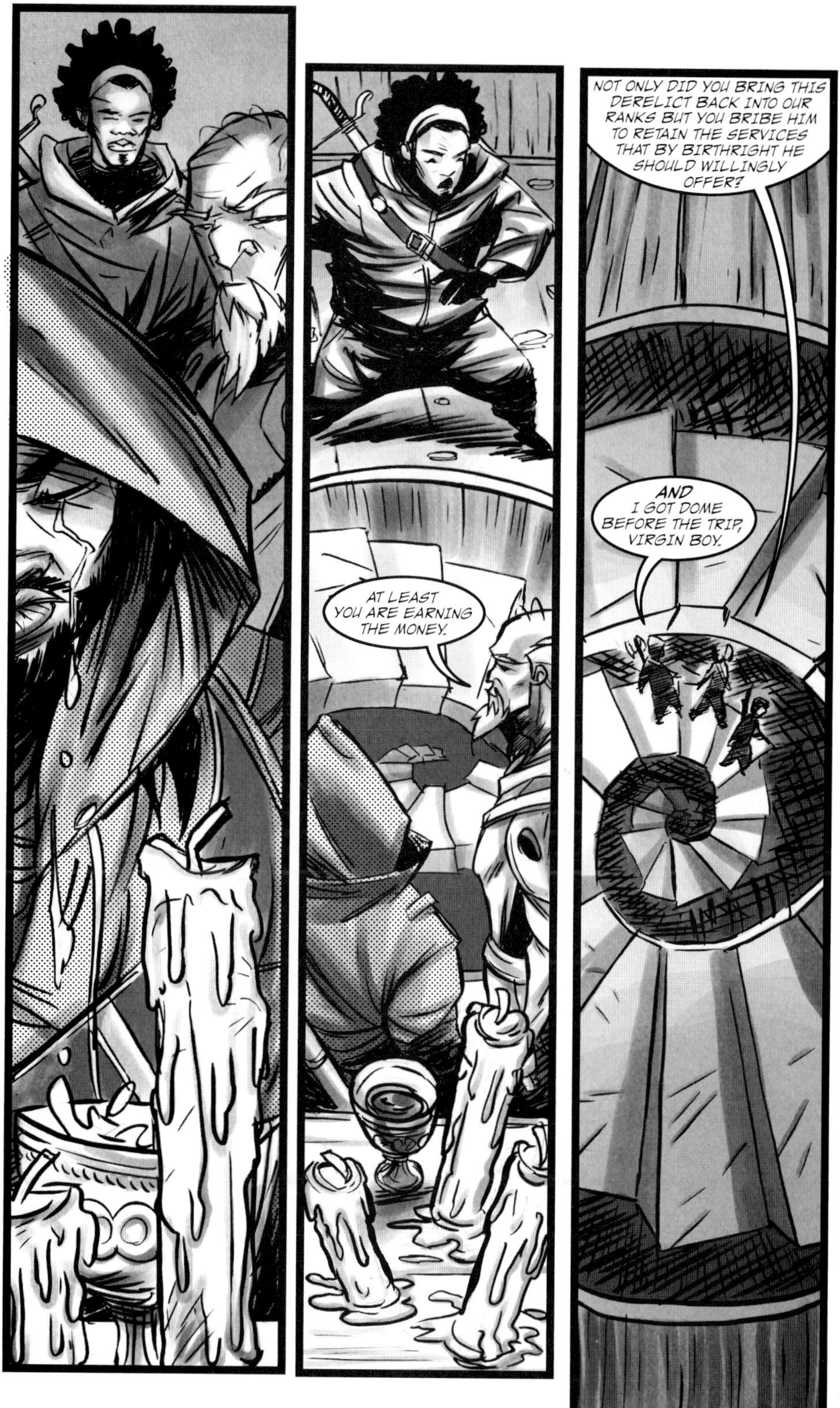
AT LEAST YOU ARE EARNING THE MONEY.
NOT ONLY DID YOU BRING THIS DERELICT BACK INTO OUR RANKS BUT YOU BRIBE HIM TO RETAIN THE SERVICES THAT BY BIRTHRIGHT HE SHOULD WILLINGLY OFFER?
AND I GOT DOME BEFORE THE TRIP, VIRGIN BOY.

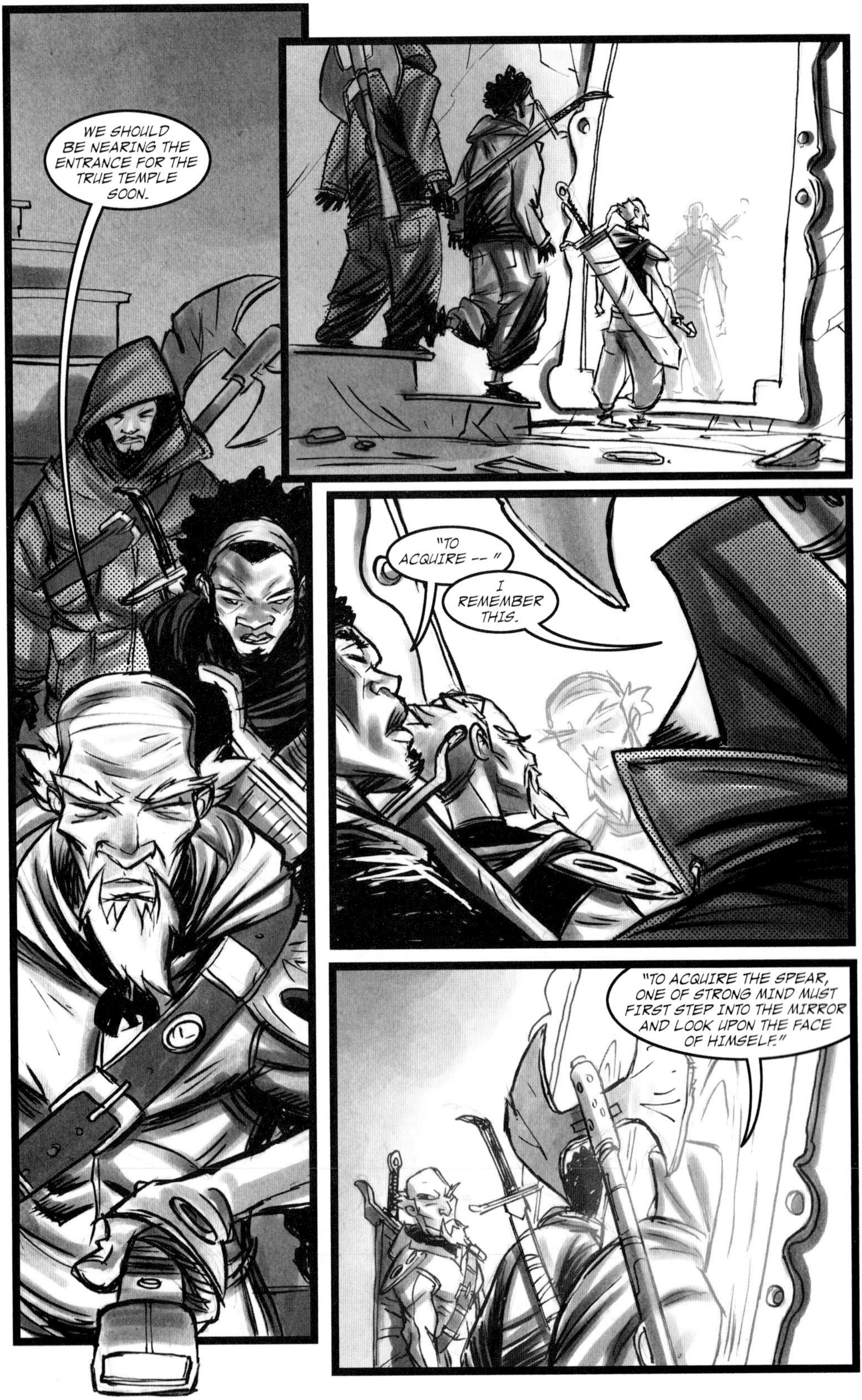
WE SHOULD BE NEARING THE ENTRANCE FOR THE TRUE TEMPLE SOON.
"TO ACQUIRE -- "
I REMEMBER THIS.
"TO ACQUIRE THE SPEAR, ONE OF STRONG MIND MUST FIRST STEP INTO THE MIRROR AND LOOK UPON THE FACE OF HIMSELF."

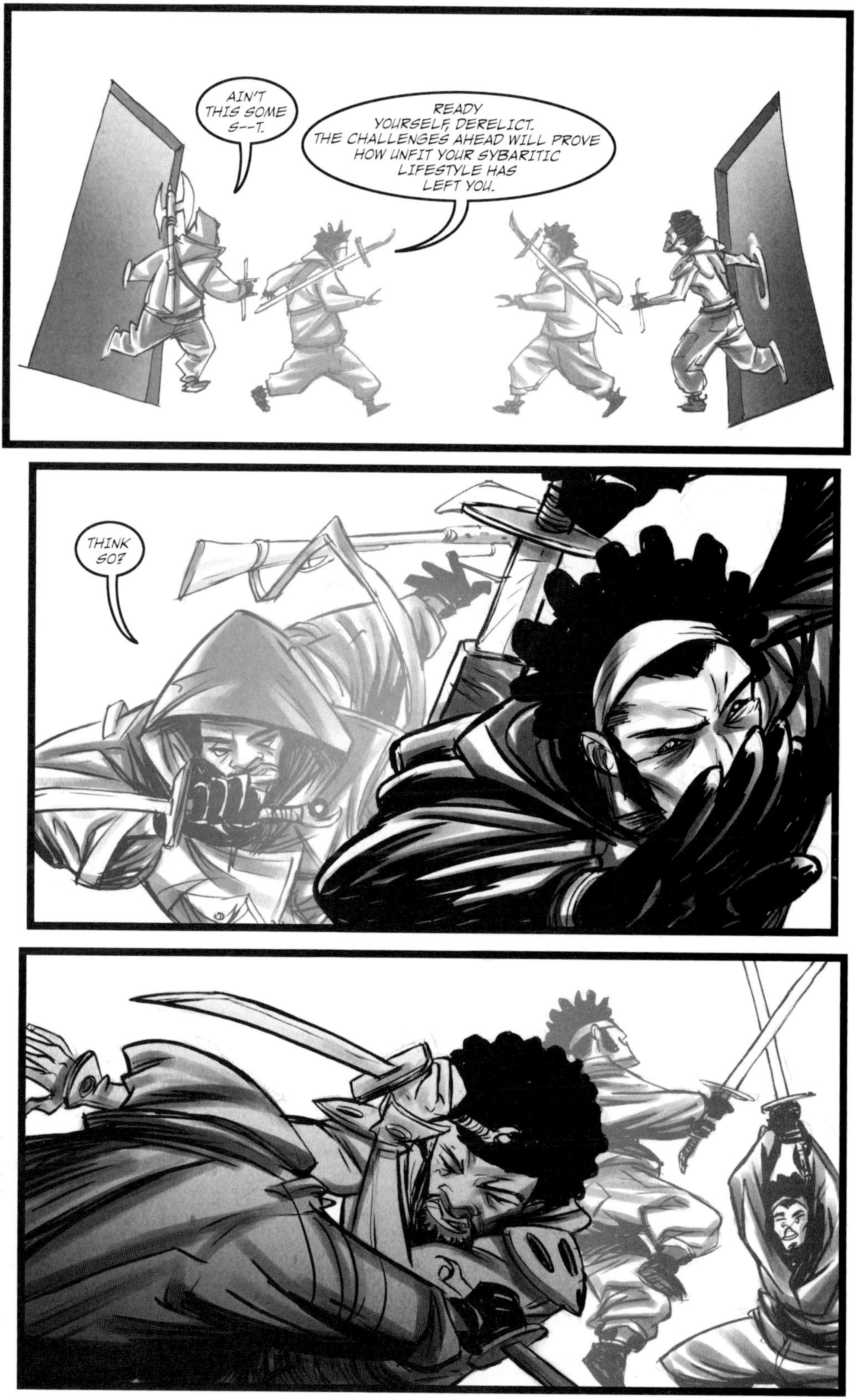
AIN'T THIS SOME S--T.
READY YOURSELF, DERELICT. THE CHALLENGES AHEAD WILL PROVE HOW UNFIT YOUR SYBARITIC LIFESTYLE HAS LEFT YOU.
THINK SO?

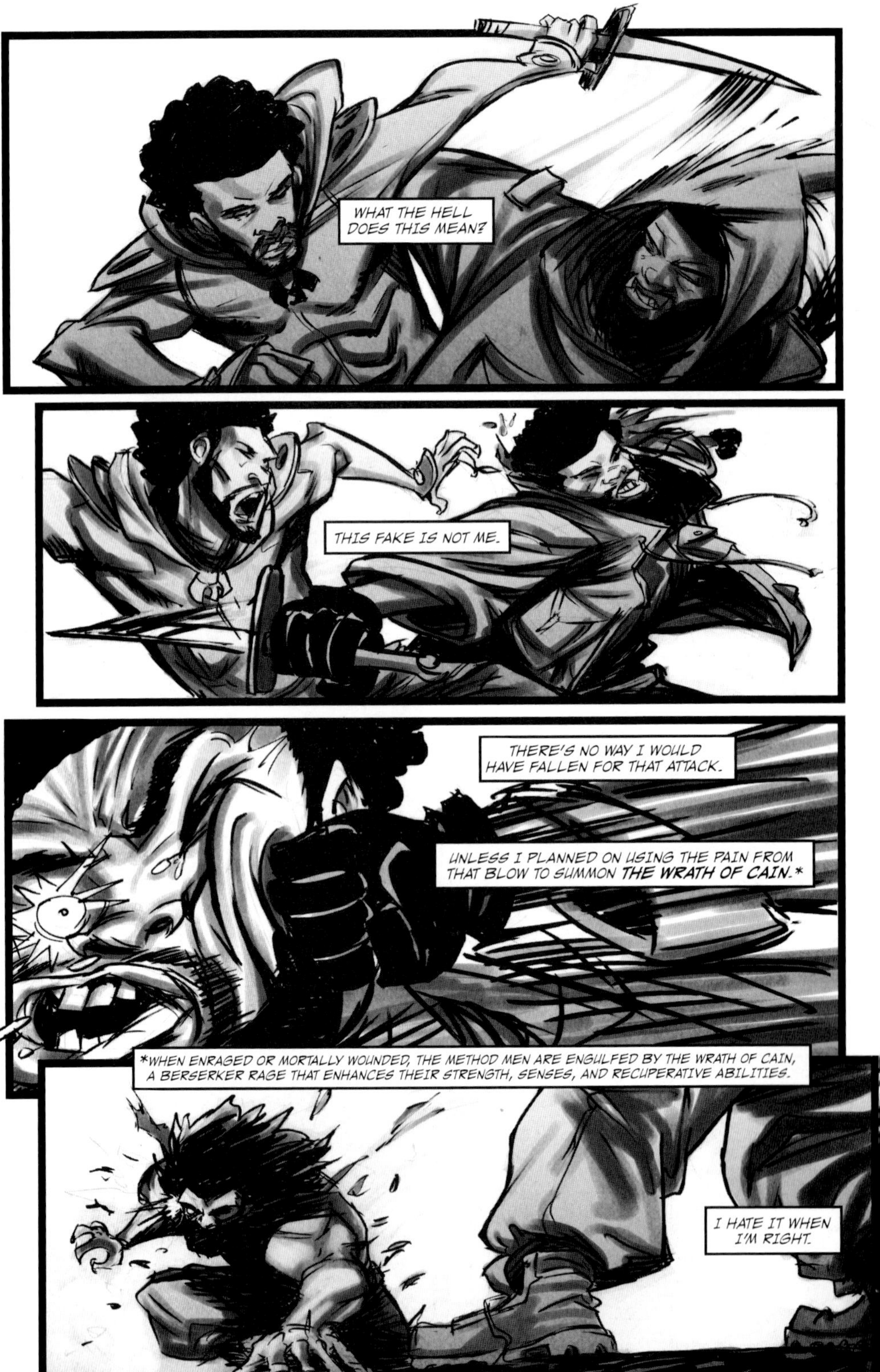
WHAT THE HELL DOES THIS MEAN?
THIS FAKE IS NOT ME.
THERE'S NO WAY I WOULD HAVE FALLEN FOR THAT ATTACK.
UNLESS I PLANNED ON USING THE PAIN FROM THAT BLOW TO SUMMON THE WRATH OF CAIN.*
*WHEN ENRAGED OR MORTALLY WOUNDED, THE METHOD MEN ARE ENGULFED BY THE WRATH OF CAIN, A BERSERKER RAGE THAT ENHANCES THEIR STRENGTH, SENSES, AND RECUPERATIVE ABILITIES.
I HATE IT WHEN I'M RIGHT.

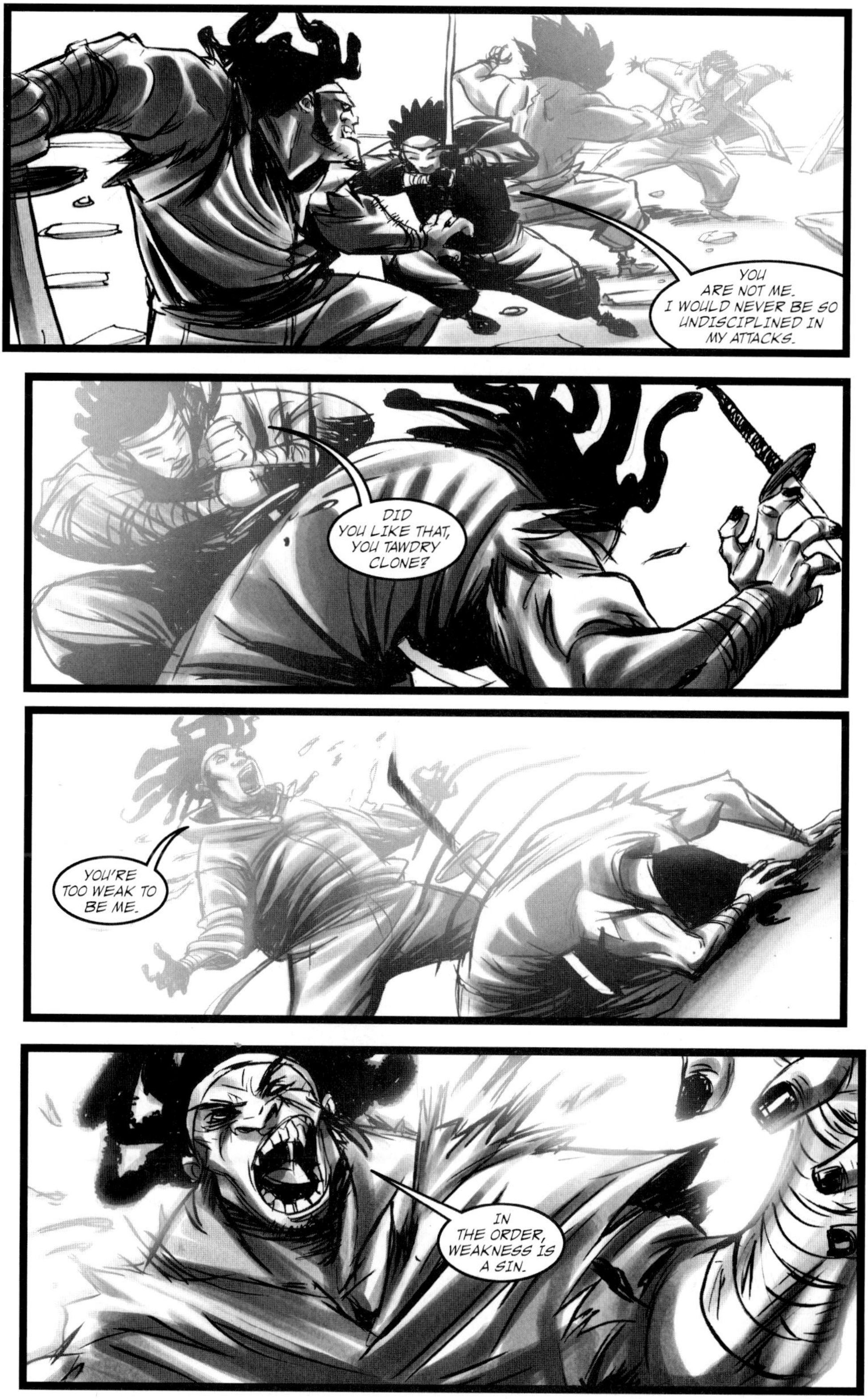
YOU ARE NOT ME. I WOULD NEVER BE SO UNDISCIPLINED IN MY ATTACKS.
DID YOU LIKE THAT, YOU TAWDRY CLONE?
YOU'RE TOO WEAK TO BE ME.
IN THE ORDER, WEAKNESS IS A SIN.

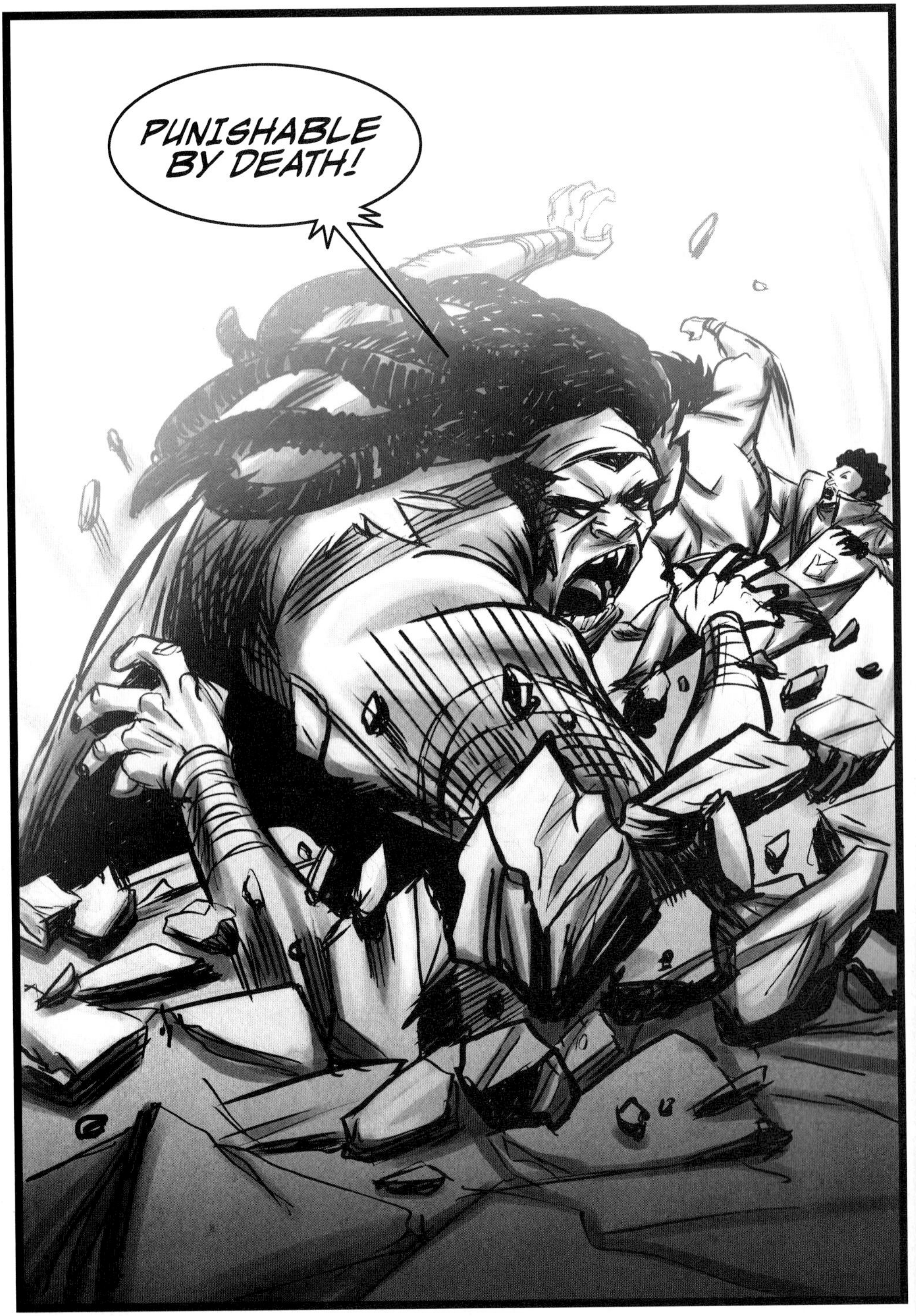
PUNISHABLE BY DEATH!

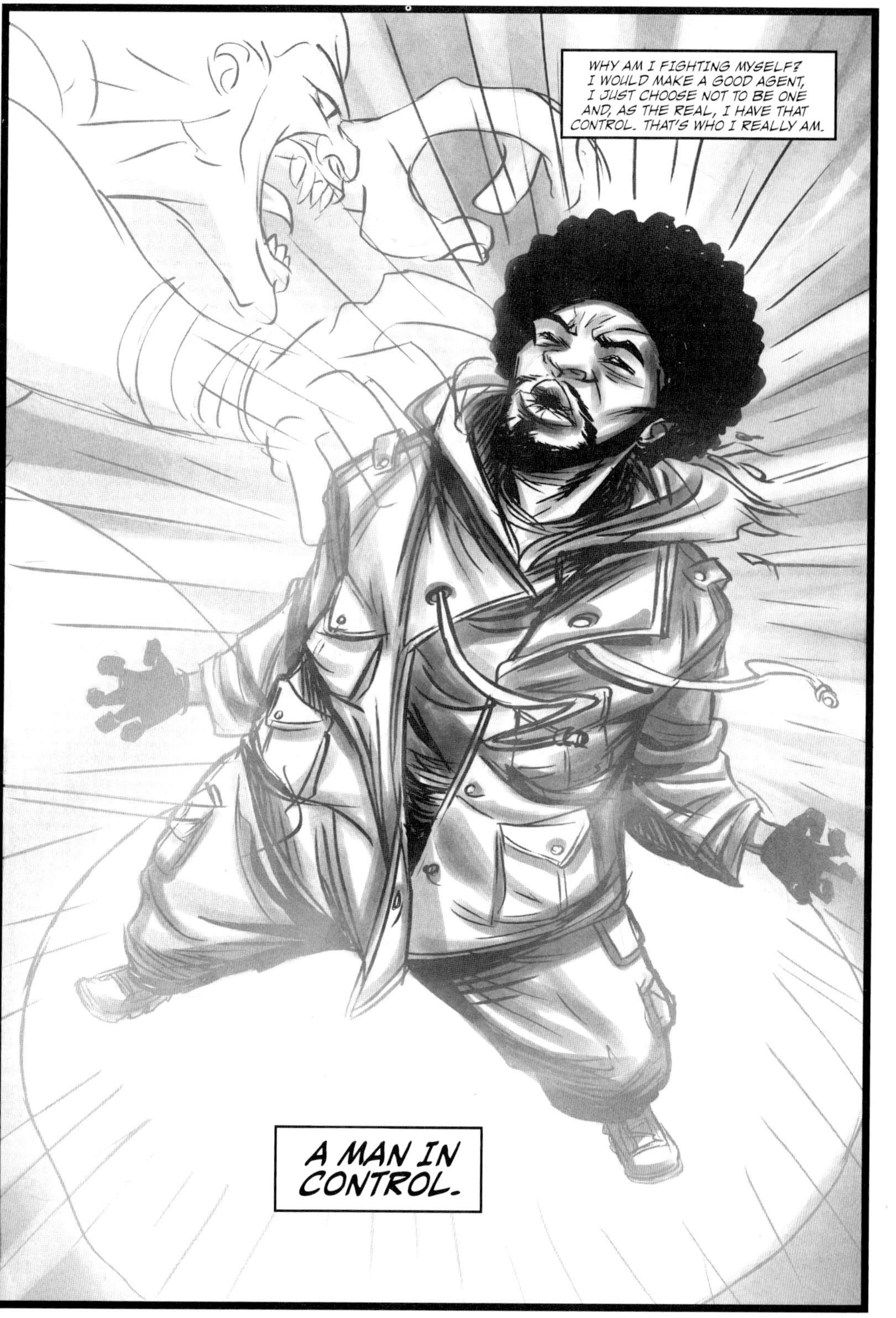
WHY AM I FIGHTING MYSELF? I WOULD MAKE A GOOD AGENT, I JUST CHOOSE NOT TO BE ONE AND, AS THE REAL, I HAVE THAT CONTROL. THAT'S WHO I REALLY AM.
A MAN IN CONTROL.

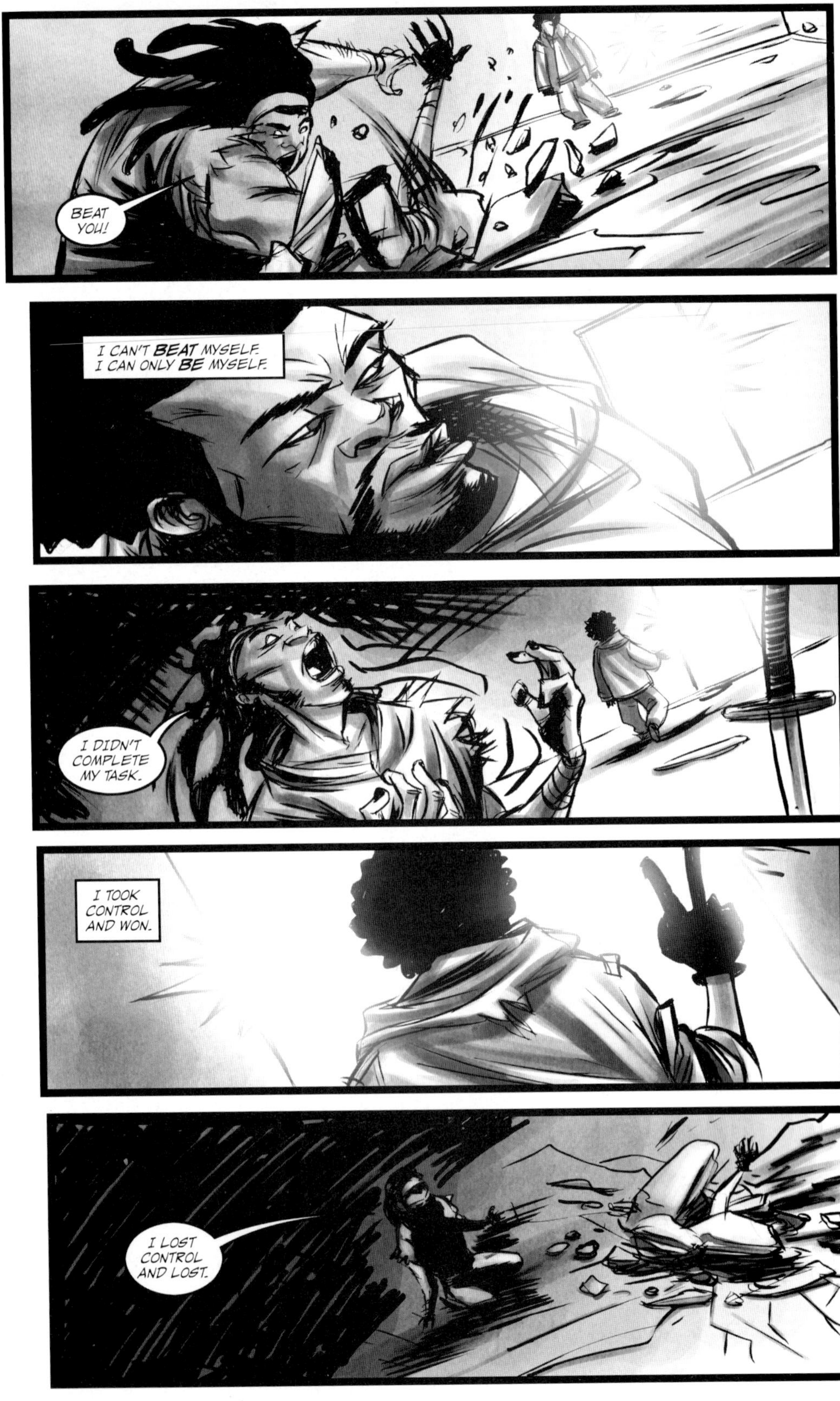
BEAT YOU!
I CAN'T BEAT MYSELF. I CAN ONLY BE MYSELF.
I DIDN'T COMPLETE MY TASK.
I TOOK CONTROL AND WON.
I LOST CONTROL AND LOST.

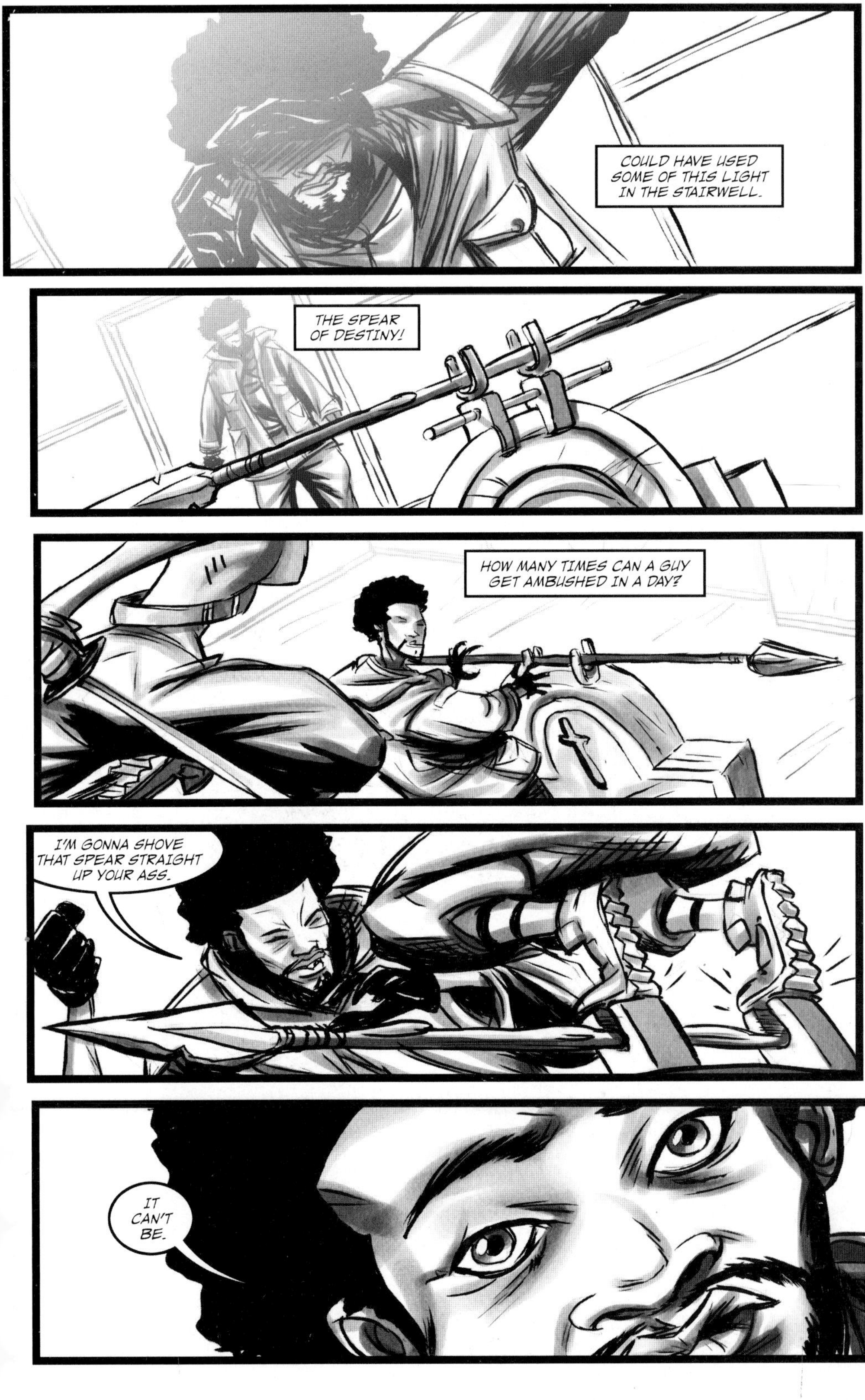
COULD HAVE USED SOME OF THIS LIGHT IN THE STAIRWELL.
THE SPEAR OF DESTINY!
HOW MANY TIMES CAN A GUY GET AMBUSHED IN A DAY?
I'M GONNA SHOVE THAT SPEAR STRAIGHT UP YOUR ASS.
IT CAN'T BE.

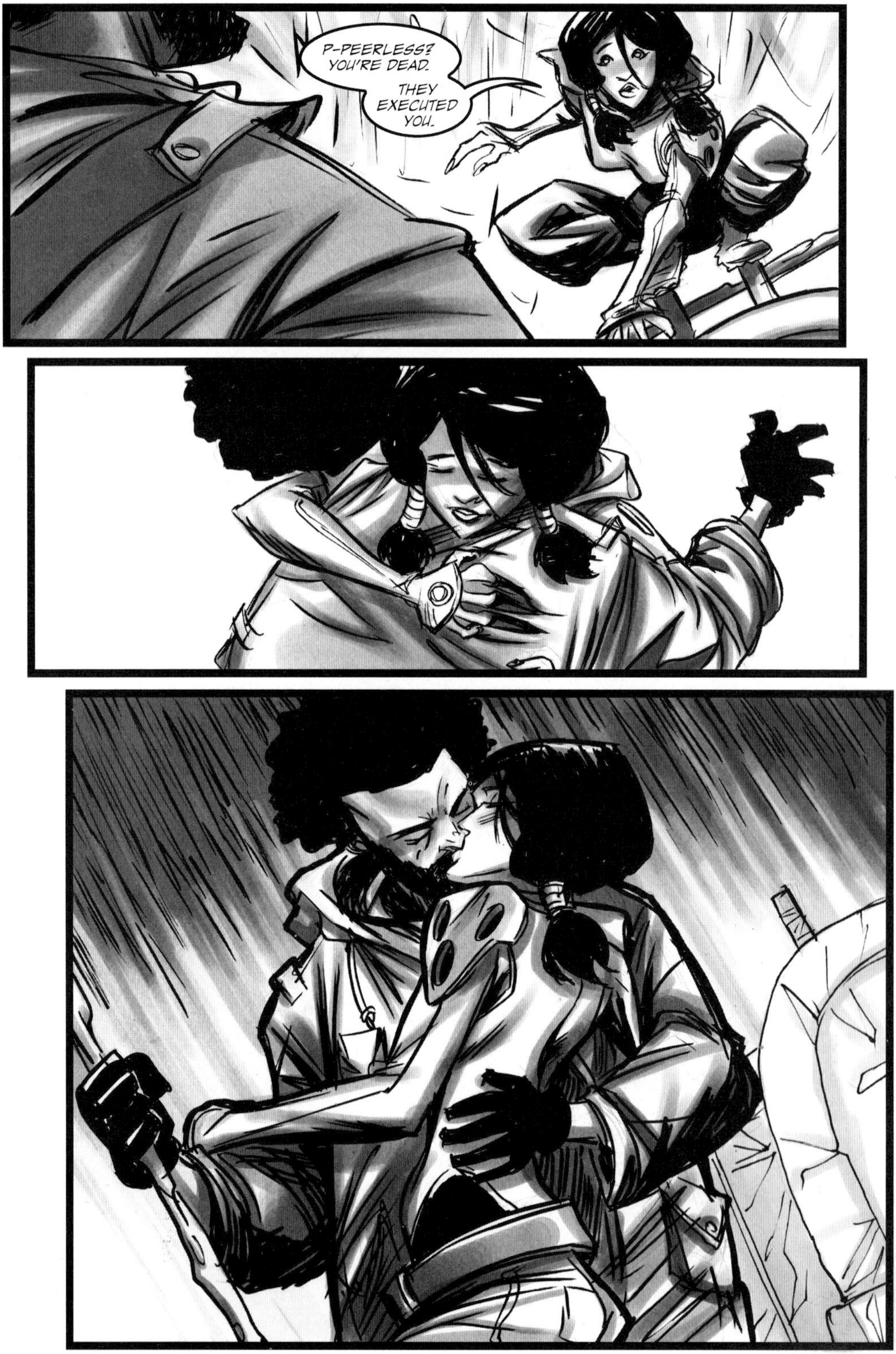
P-PEERLESS? YOU'RE DEAD.
THEY EXECUTED YOU.

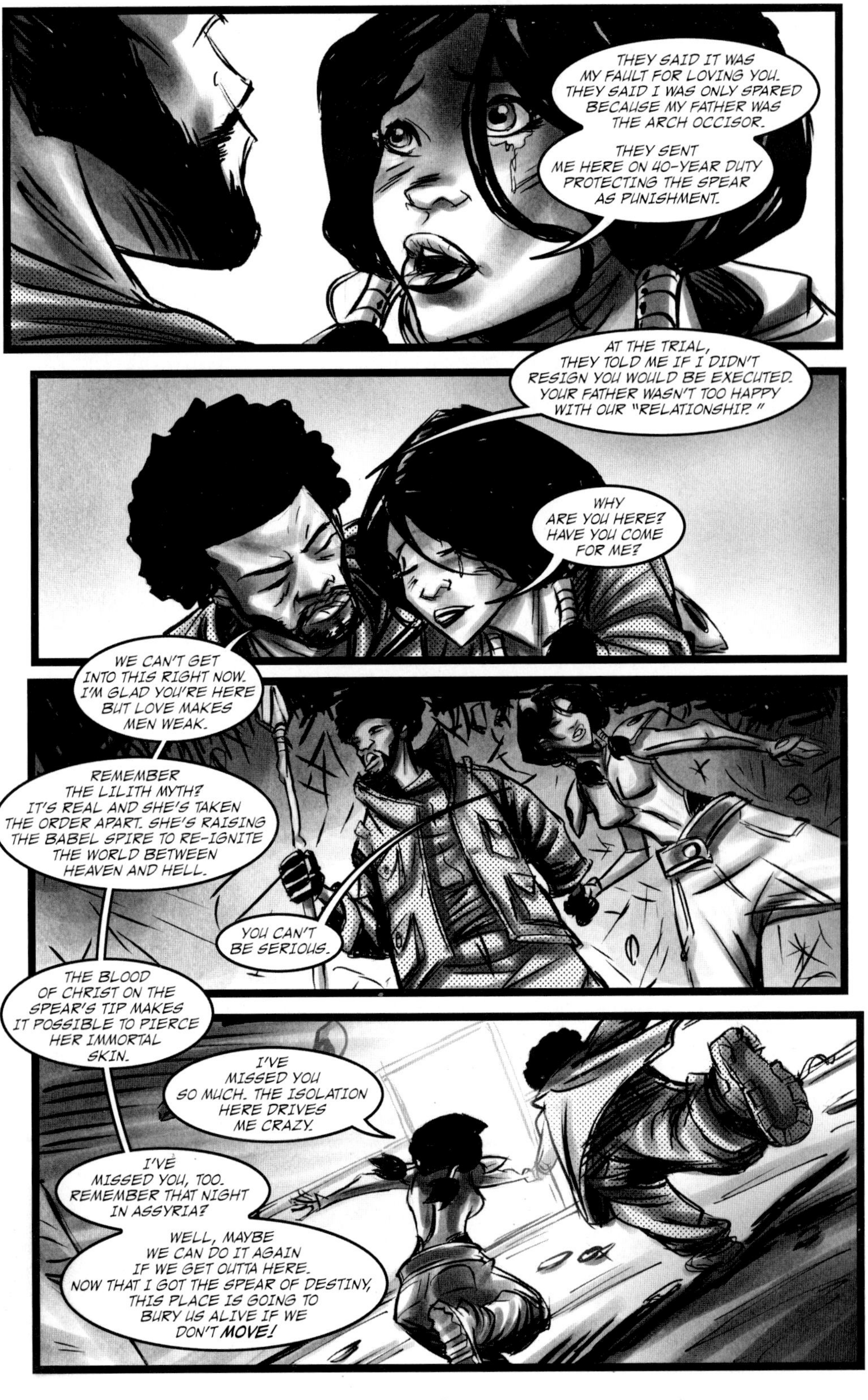
THEY SAID IT WAS MY FAULT FOR LOVING YOU. THEY SAID I WAS ONLY SPARED BECAUSE MY FATHER WAS THE ARCH OCCISOR.
THEY SENT ME HERE ON 40-YEAR DUTY PROTECTING THE SPEAR AS PUNISHMENT.
AT THE TRIAL, THEY TOLD ME IF I DIDN'T RESIGN YOU WOULD BE EXECUTED. YOUR FATHER WASN'T TOO HAPPY WITH OUR "RELATIONSHIP."
WHY ARE YOU HERE? HAVE YOU COME FOR ME?
WE CAN'T GET INTO THIS RIGHT NOW. I'M GLAD YOU'RE HERE BUT LOVE MAKES MEN WEAK.
REMEMBER THE LILITH MYTH? IT'S REAL AND SHE'S TAKEN THE ORDER APART. SHE'S RAISING THE BABEL SPIRE TO RE-IGNITE THE WORLD BETWEEN HEAVEN AND HELL.
YOU CAN'T BE SERIOUS.
THE BLOOD OF CHRIST ON THE SPEAR'S TIP MAKES IT POSSIBLE TO PIERCE HER IMMORTAL SKIN.
I'VE MISSED YOU SO MUCH. THE ISOLATION HERE DRIVES ME CRAZY.
I'VE MISSED YOU, TOO. REMEMBER THAT NIGHT IN ASSYRIA?
WELL, MAYBE WE CAN DO IT AGAIN IF WE GET OUTTA HERE. NOW THAT I GOT THE SPEAR OF DESTINY, THIS PLACE IS GOING TO BURY US ALIVE IF WE DON'T **MOVE!**

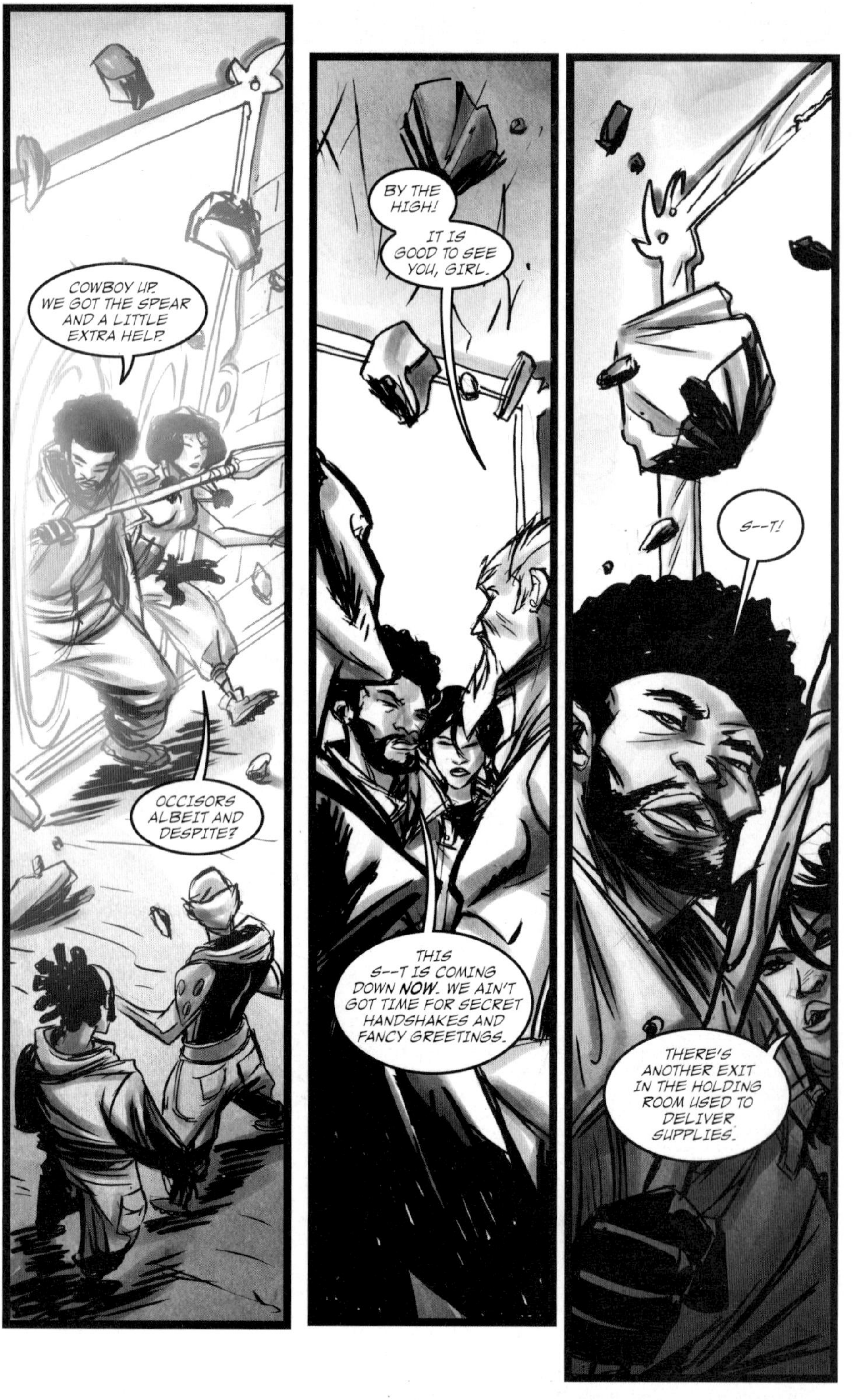
COWBOY UP. WE GOT THE SPEAR AND A LITTLE EXTRA HELP.
OCCISORS ALBEIT AND DESPITE?
BY THE HIGH!
IT IS GOOD TO SEE YOU, GIRL.
THIS S--T IS COMING DOWN NOW. WE AIN'T GOT TIME FOR SECRET HANDSHAKES AND FANCY GREETINGS.
S--T!
THERE'S ANOTHER EXIT IN THE HOLDING ROOM USED TO DELIVER SUPPLIES.

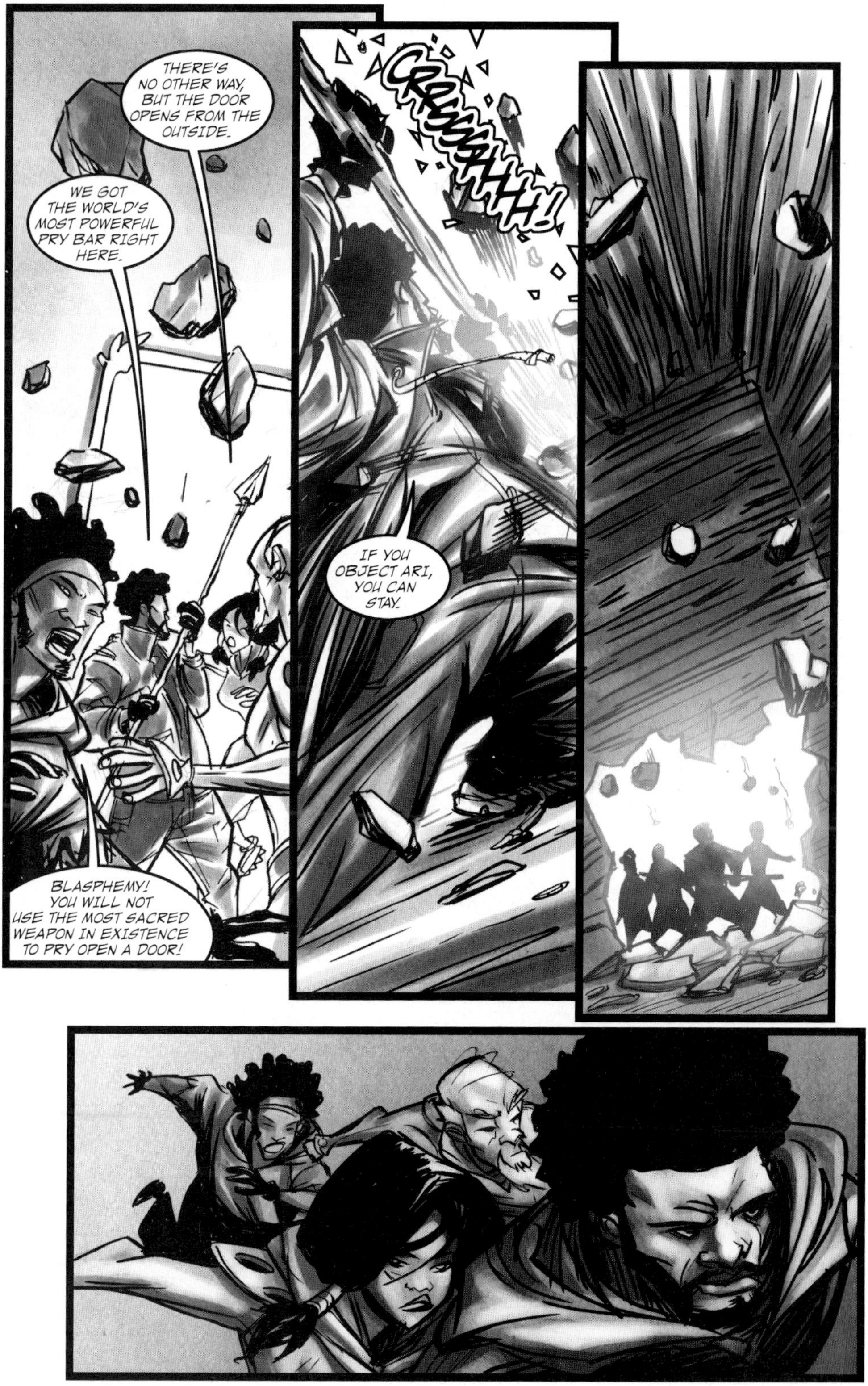
THERE'S NO OTHER WAY, BUT THE DOOR OPENS FROM THE OUTSIDE.
WE GOT THE WORLD'S MOST POWERFUL PRY BAR RIGHT HERE.
BLASPHEMY! YOU WILL NOT USE THE MOST SACRED WEAPON IN EXISTENCE TO PRY OPEN A DOOR!
CRRSSSSHHHH!
IF YOU OBJECT ARI, YOU CAN STAY.

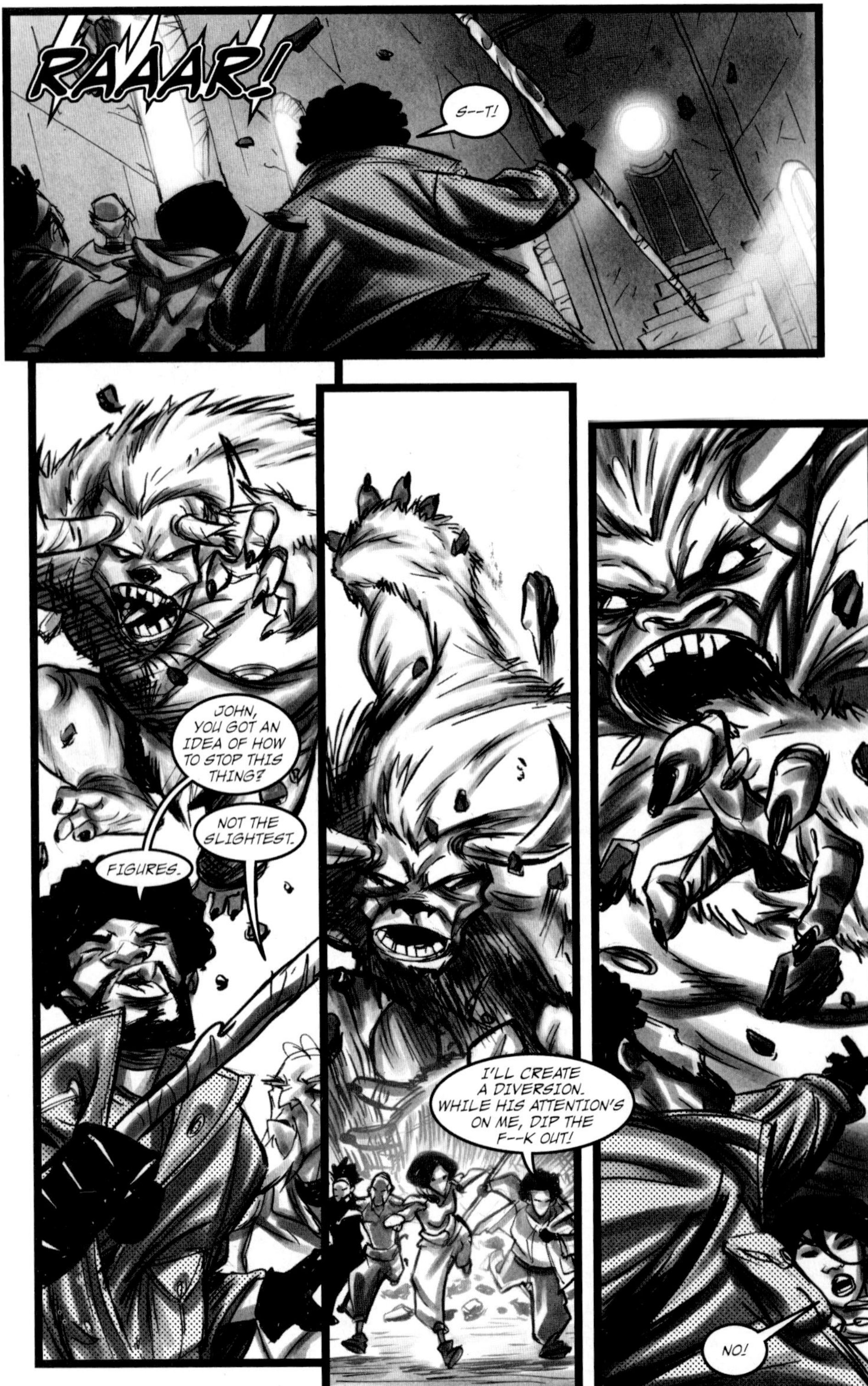
RAAAR!
S--T!
JOHN, YOU GOT AN IDEA OF HOW TO STOP THIS THING?
NOT THE SLIGHTEST.
FIGURES.
I'LL CREATE A DIVERSION. WHILE HIS ATTENTION'S ON ME, DIP THE F--K OUT!
NO!

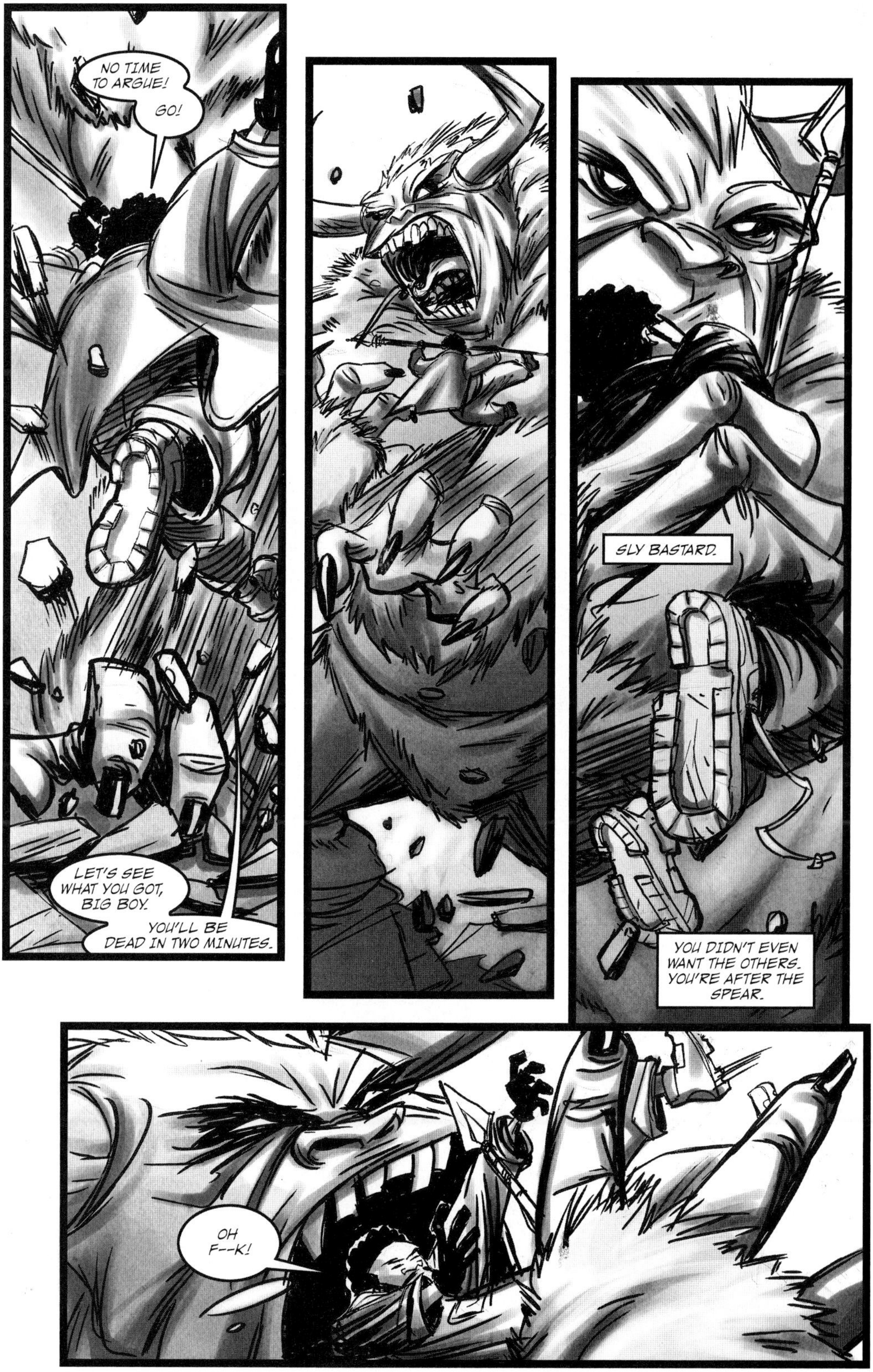
NO TIME TO ARGUE!
GO!
LET'S SEE WHAT YOU GOT, BIG BOY.
YOU'LL BE DEAD IN TWO MINUTES.
SLY BASTARD.
YOU DIDN'T EVEN WANT THE OTHERS. YOU'RE AFTER THE SPEAR.
OH F--K!

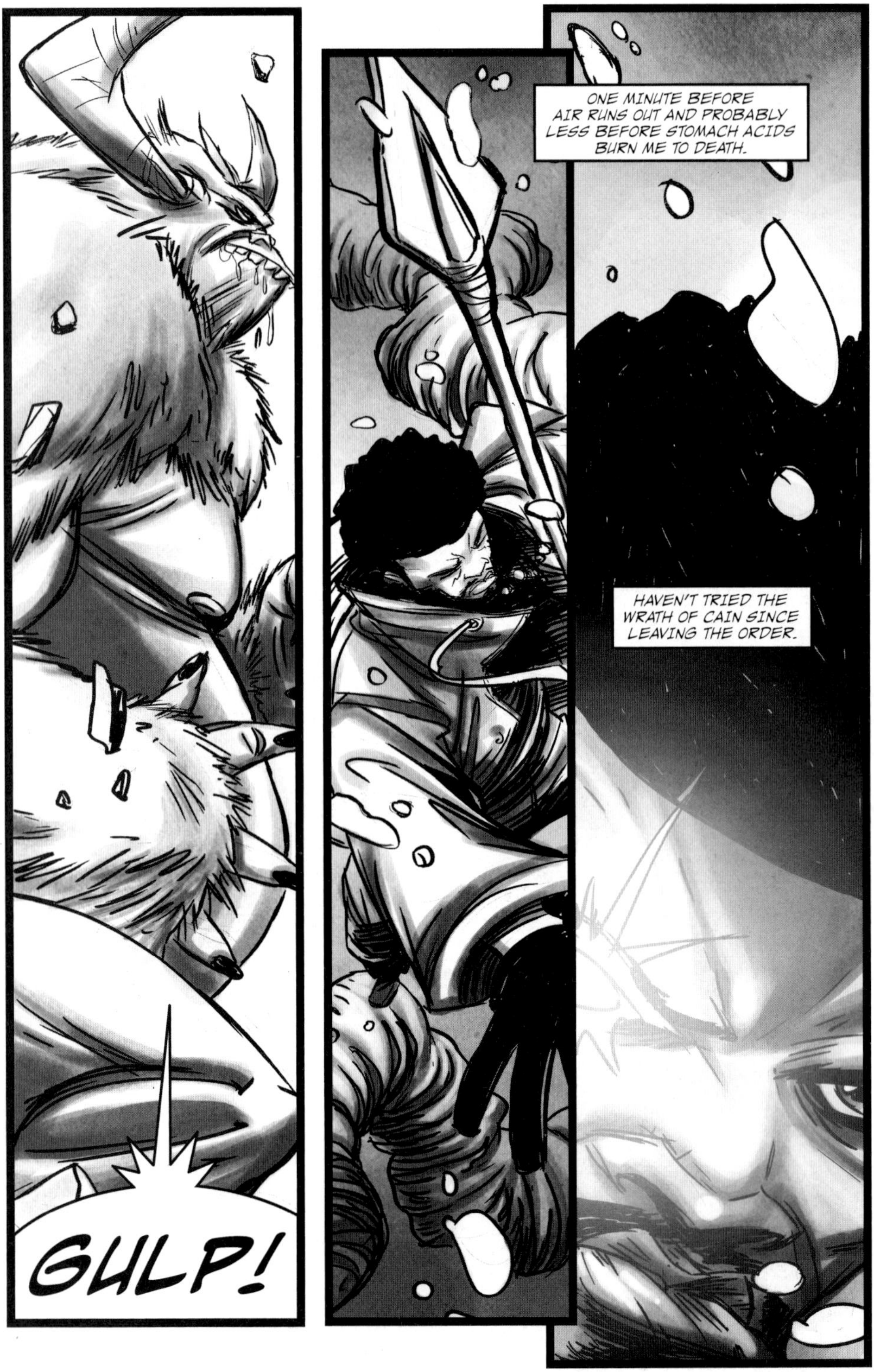
GULP!
ONE MINUTE BEFORE AIR RUNS OUT AND PROBABLY LESS BEFORE STOMACH ACIDS BURN ME TO DEATH.
HAVEN'T TRIED THE WRATH OF CAIN SINCE LEAVING THE ORDER.

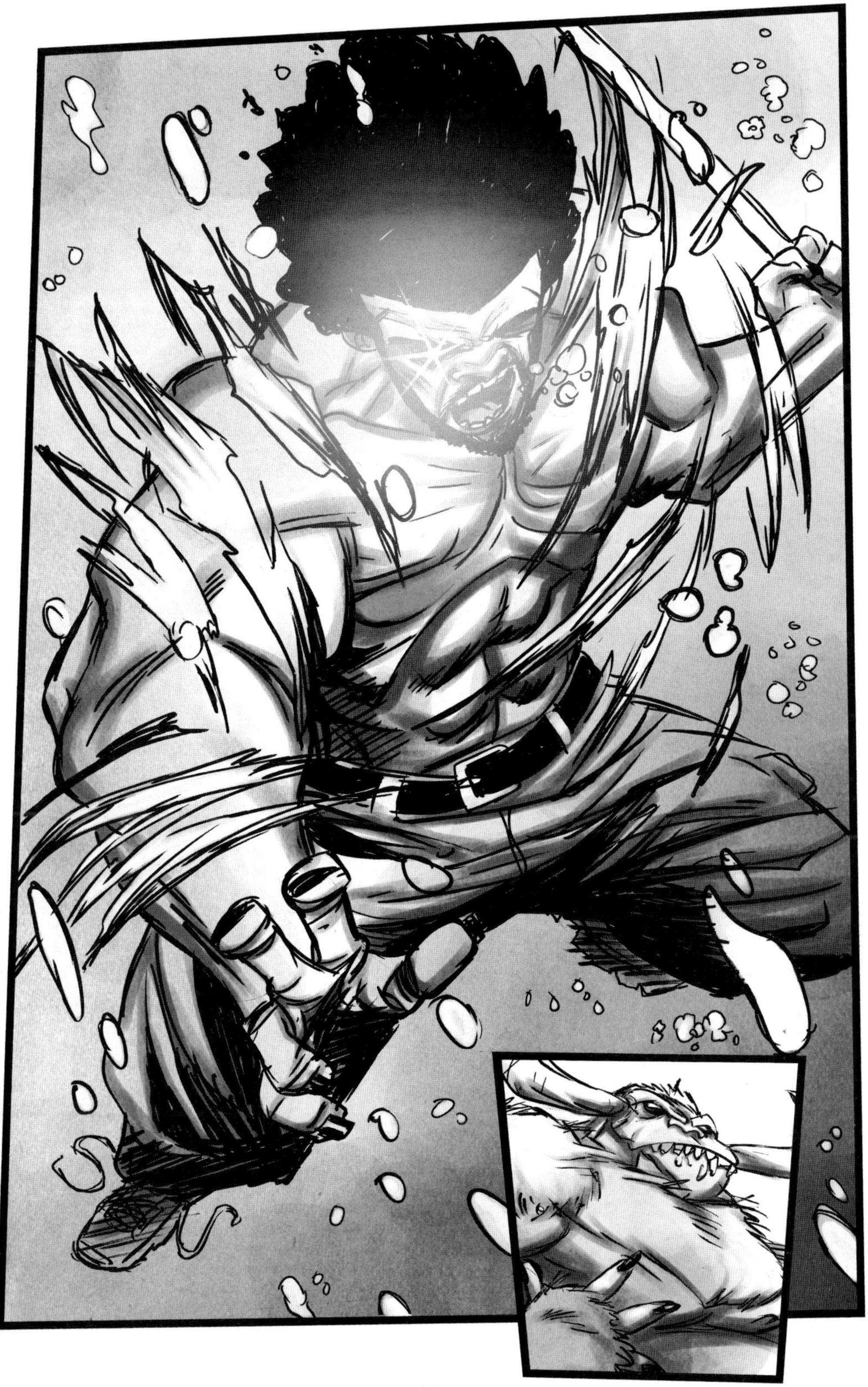

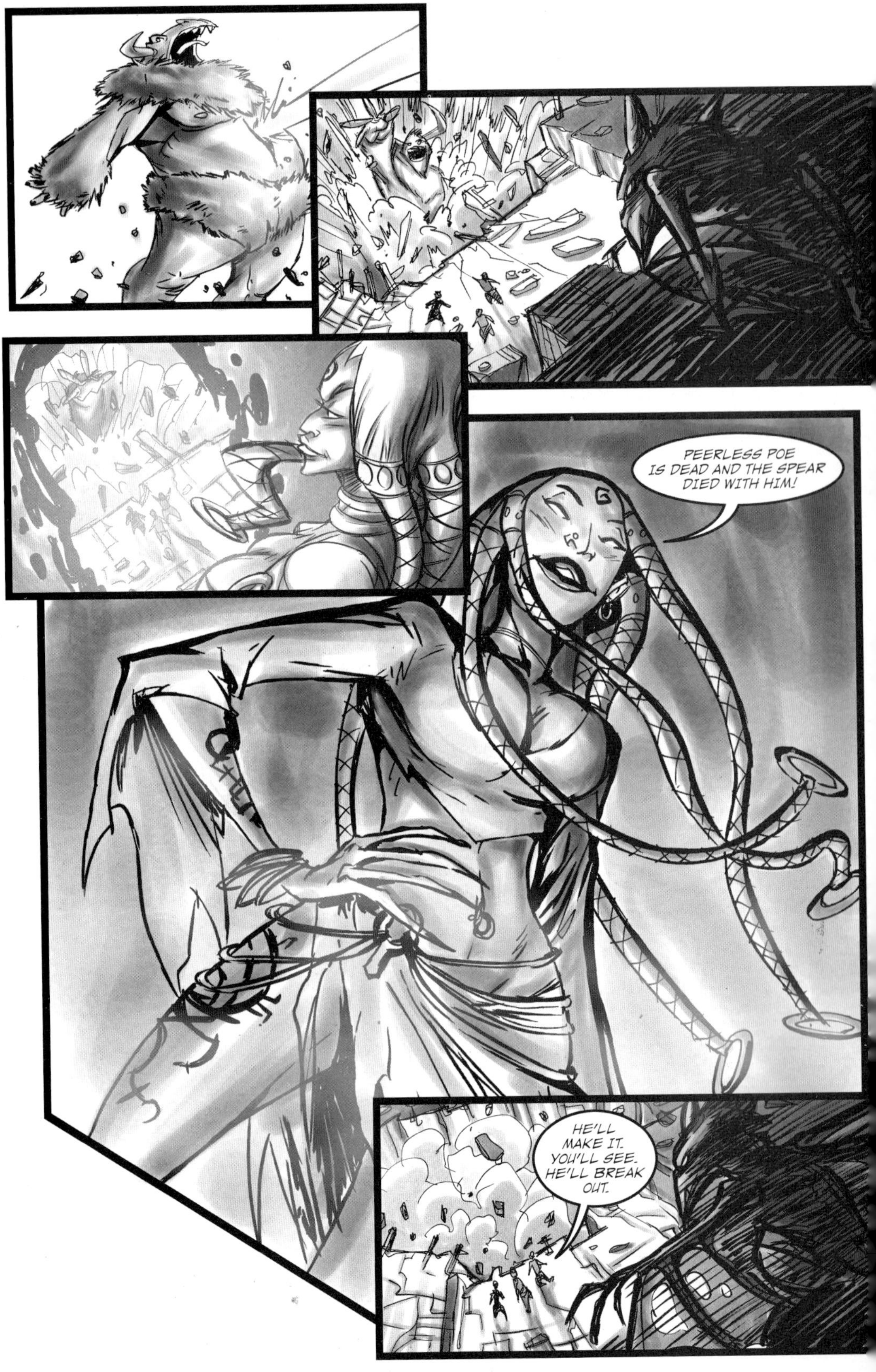
PEERLESS POE
IS DEAD AND THE SPEAR
DIED WITH HIM!
HE'LL MAKE IT. YOU'LL SEE. HE'LL BREAK OUT.

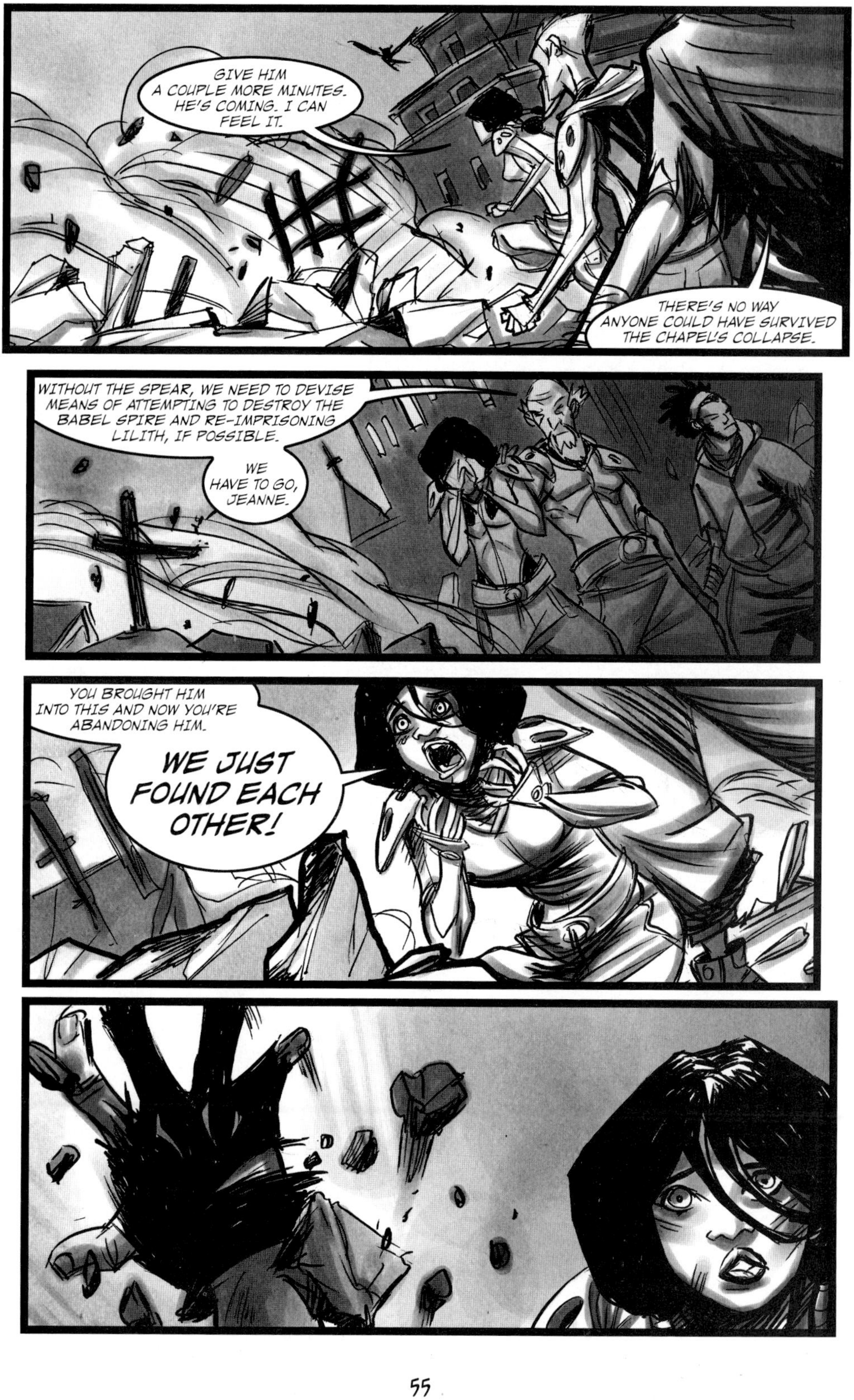
GIVE HIM A COUPLE MORE MINUTES. HE'S COMING. I CAN FEEL IT.
THERE'S NO WAY ANYONE COULD HAVE SURVIVED THE CHAPEL'S COLLAPSE.
WITHOUT THE SPEAR, WE NEED TO DEVISE MEANS OF ATTEMPTING TO DESTROY THE BABEL SPIRE AND RE-IMPRISONING LILITH, IF POSSIBLE.
WE HAVE TO GO, JEANNE.
YOU BROUGHT HIM INTO THIS AND NOW YOU'RE ABANDONING HIM.
WE JUST FOUND EACH OTHER!

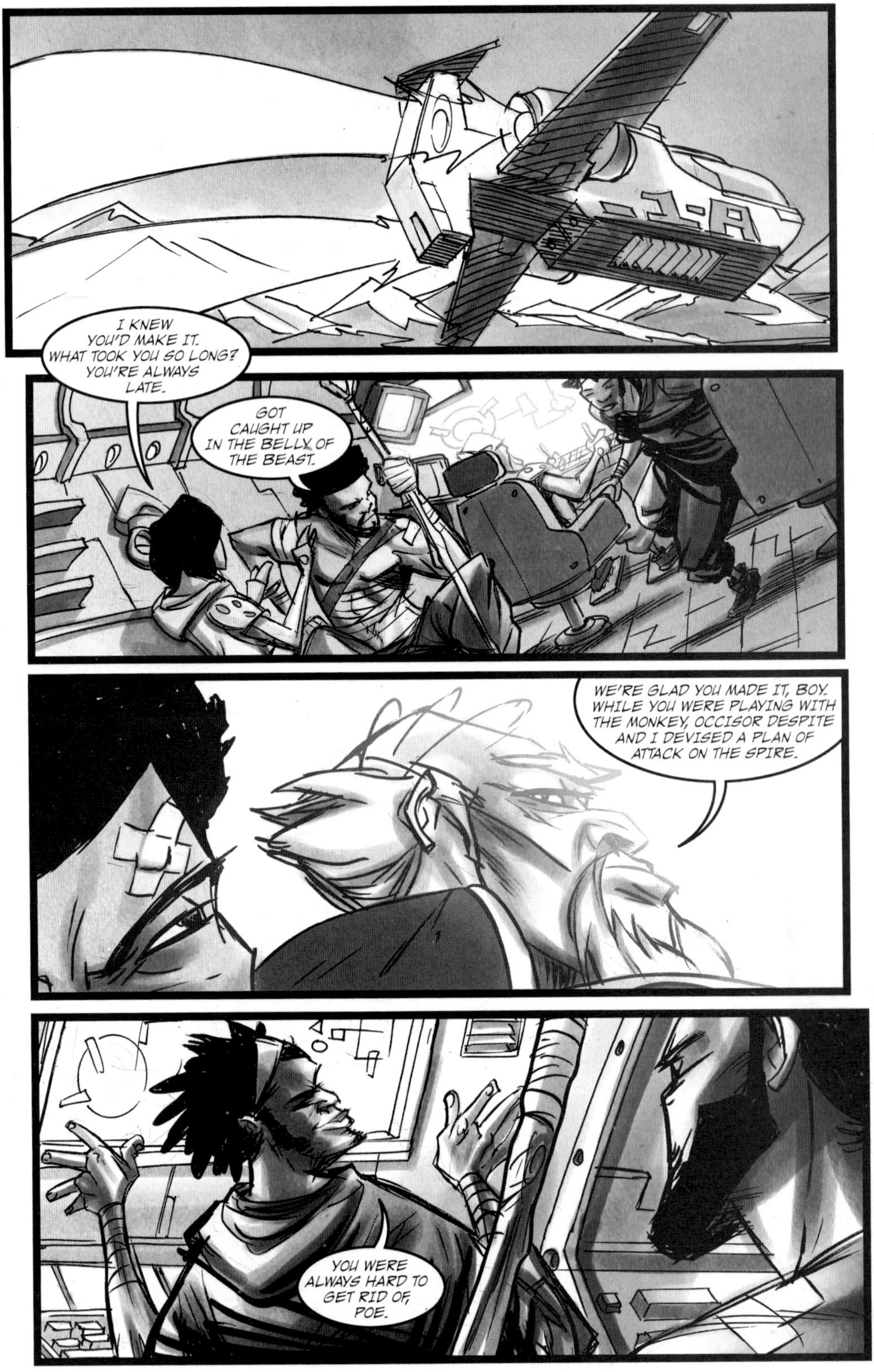
I KNEW YOU'D MAKE IT. WHAT TOOK YOU SO LONG? YOU'RE ALWAYS LATE.
GOT CAUGHT UP IN THE BELLY OF THE BEAST.
WE'RE GLAD YOU MADE IT, BOY. WHILE YOU WERE PLAYING WITH THE MONKEY, OCCISOR DESPITE AND I DEVISED A PLAN OF ATTACK ON THE SPIRE.
YOU WERE ALWAYS HARD TO GET RID OF, POE.

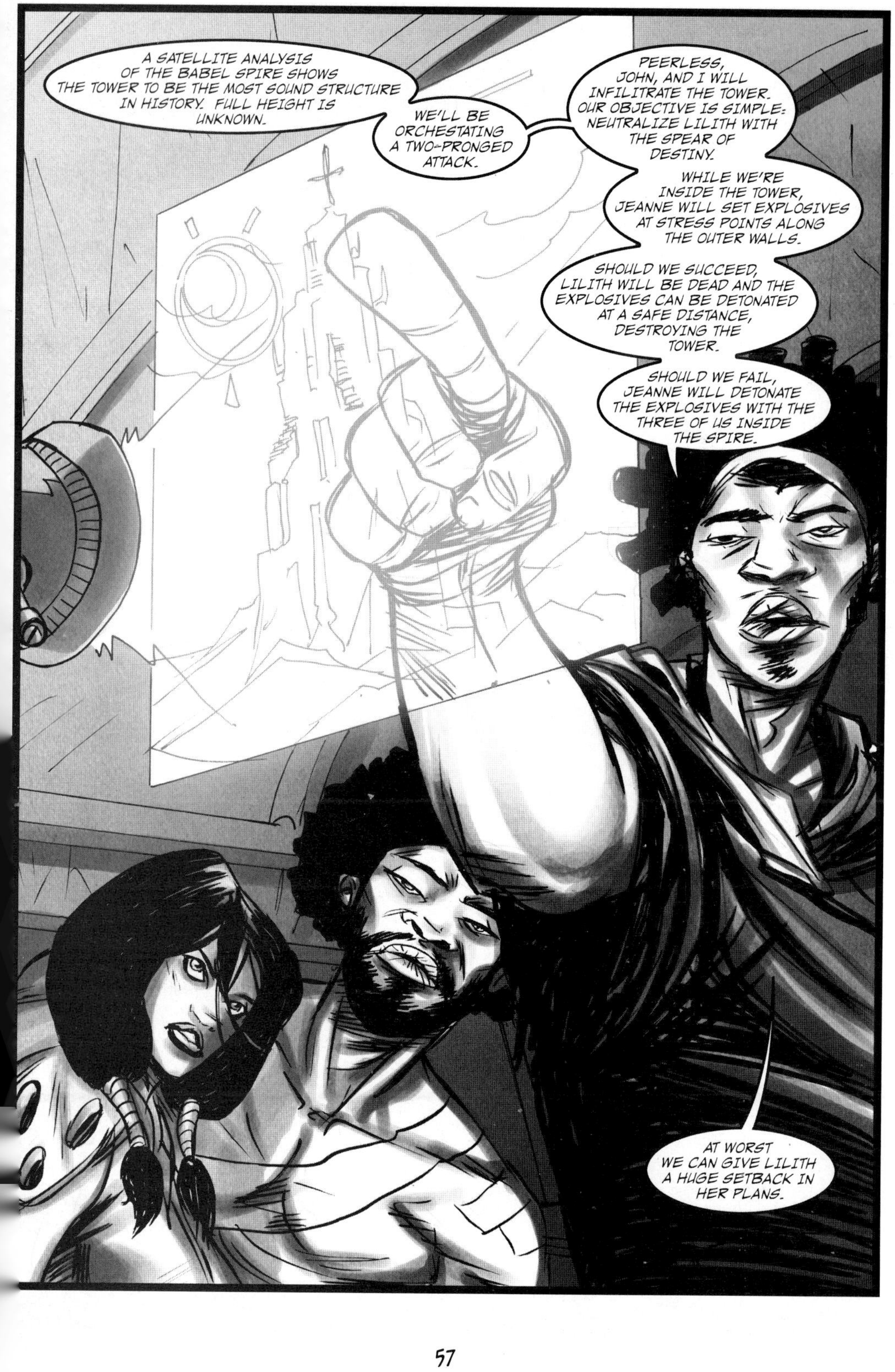
A SATELLITE ANALYSIS OF THE BABEL SPIRE SHOWS THE TOWER TO BE THE MOST SOUND STRUCTURE IN HISTORY. FULL HEIGHT IS UNKNOWN.
WE'LL BE ORCHESTATING A TWO-PRONGED ATTACK.
PEERLESS, JOHN, AND I WILL INFILITRATE THE TOWER. OUR OBJECTIVE IS SIMPLE: NEUTRALIZE LILITH WITH THE SPEAR OF DESTINY.
WHILE WE'RE INSIDE THE TOWER, JEANNE WILL SET EXPLOSIVES AT STRESS POINTS ALONG THE OUTER WALLS.
SHOULD WE SUCCEED, LILITH WILL BE DEAD AND THE EXPLOSIVES CAN BE DETONATED AT A SAFE DISTANCE, DESTROYING THE TOWER.
SHOULD WE FAIL, JEANNE WILL DETONATE THE EXPLOSIVES WITH THE THREE OF US INSIDE THE SPIRE.
AT WORST WE CAN GIVE LILITH A HUGE SETBACK IN HER PLANS.

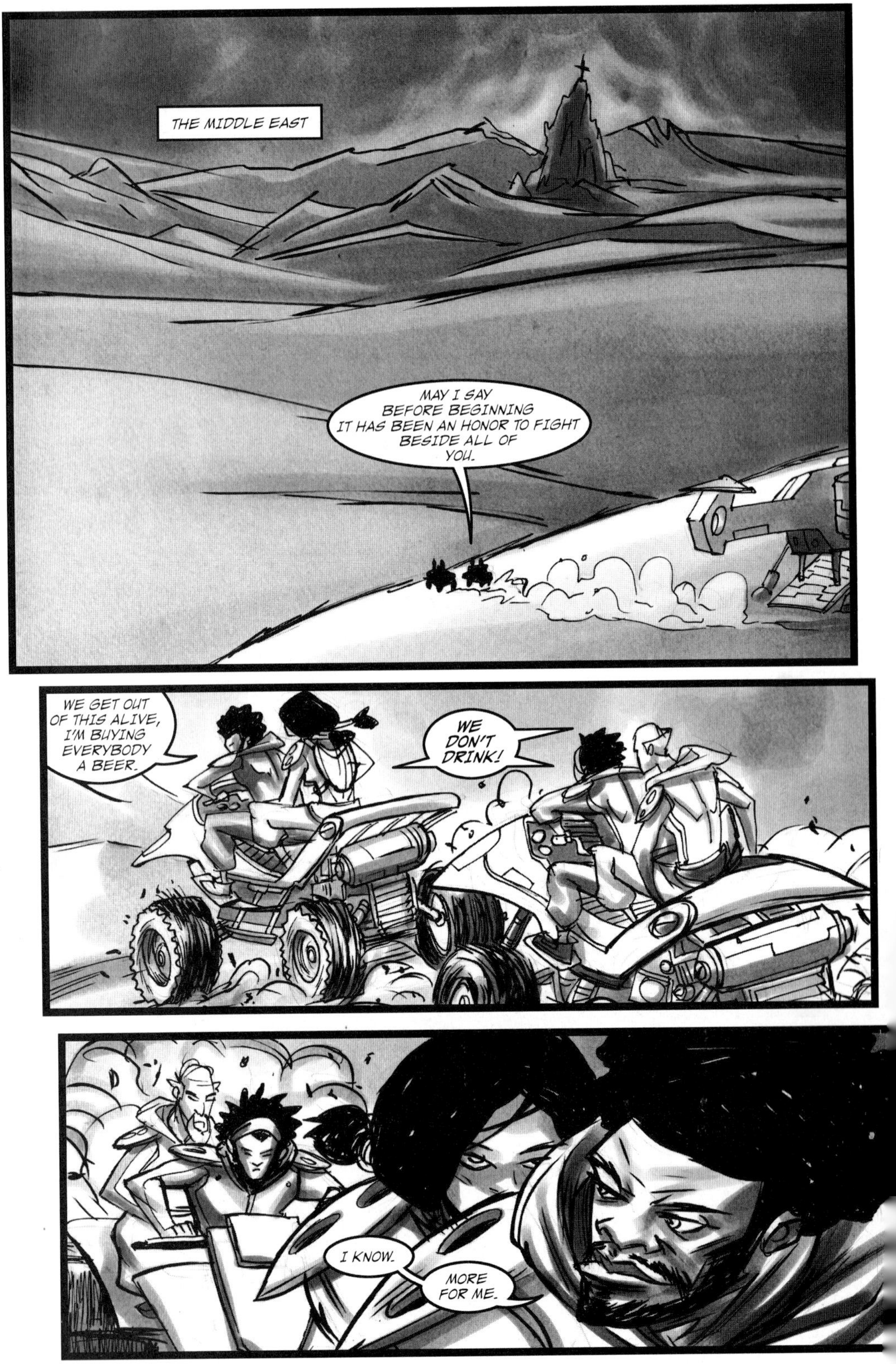
THE MIDDLE EAST
MAY I SAY BEFORE BEGINNING IT HAS BEEN AN HONOR TO FIGHT BESIDE ALL OF YOU.
WE GET OUT OF THIS ALIVE, I'M BUYING EVERYBODY A BEER.
WE DON'T DRINK!
I KNOW.
MORE FOR ME.

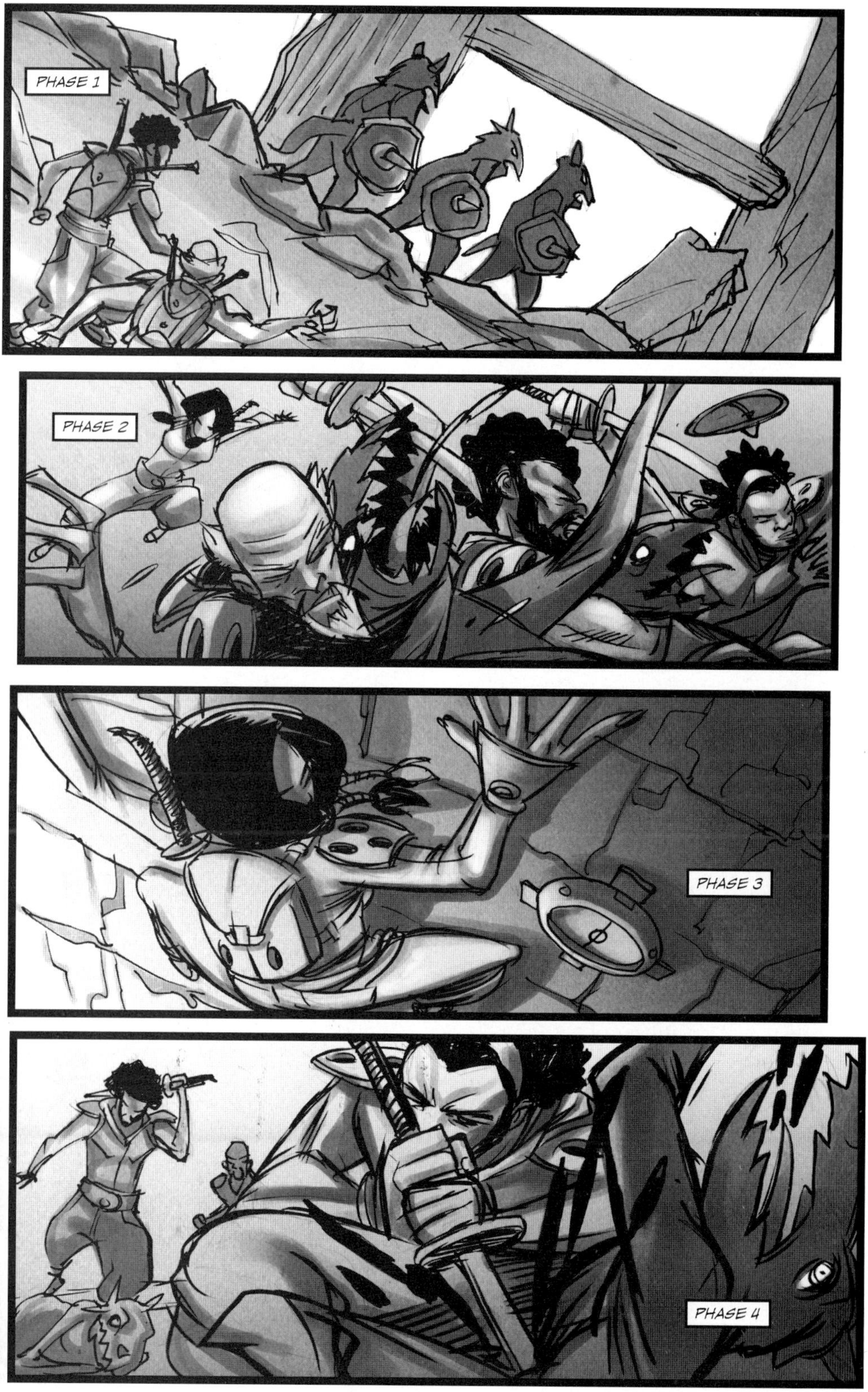
PHASE 1
PHASE 2
PHASE 3
PHASE 4

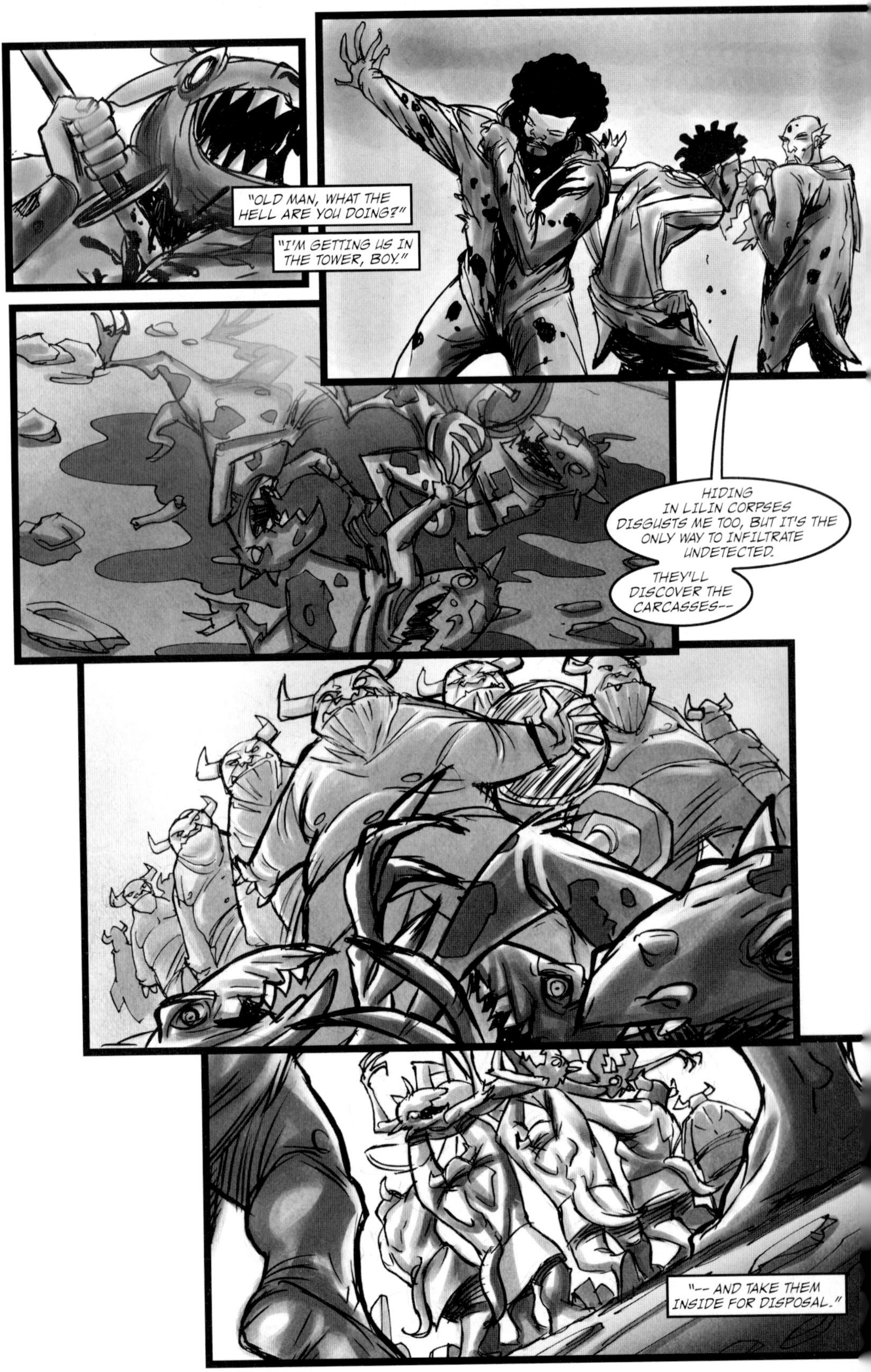
"OLD MAN, WHAT THE HELL ARE YOU DOING?"
"I'M GETTING US IN THE TOWER, BOY."
HIDING IN LILIN CORPSES DISGUSTS ME TOO, BUT IT'S THE ONLY WAY TO INFILTRATE UNDETECTED.
THEY'LL DISCOVER THE CARCASSES--
"-- AND TAKE THEM INSIDE FOR DISPOSAL."

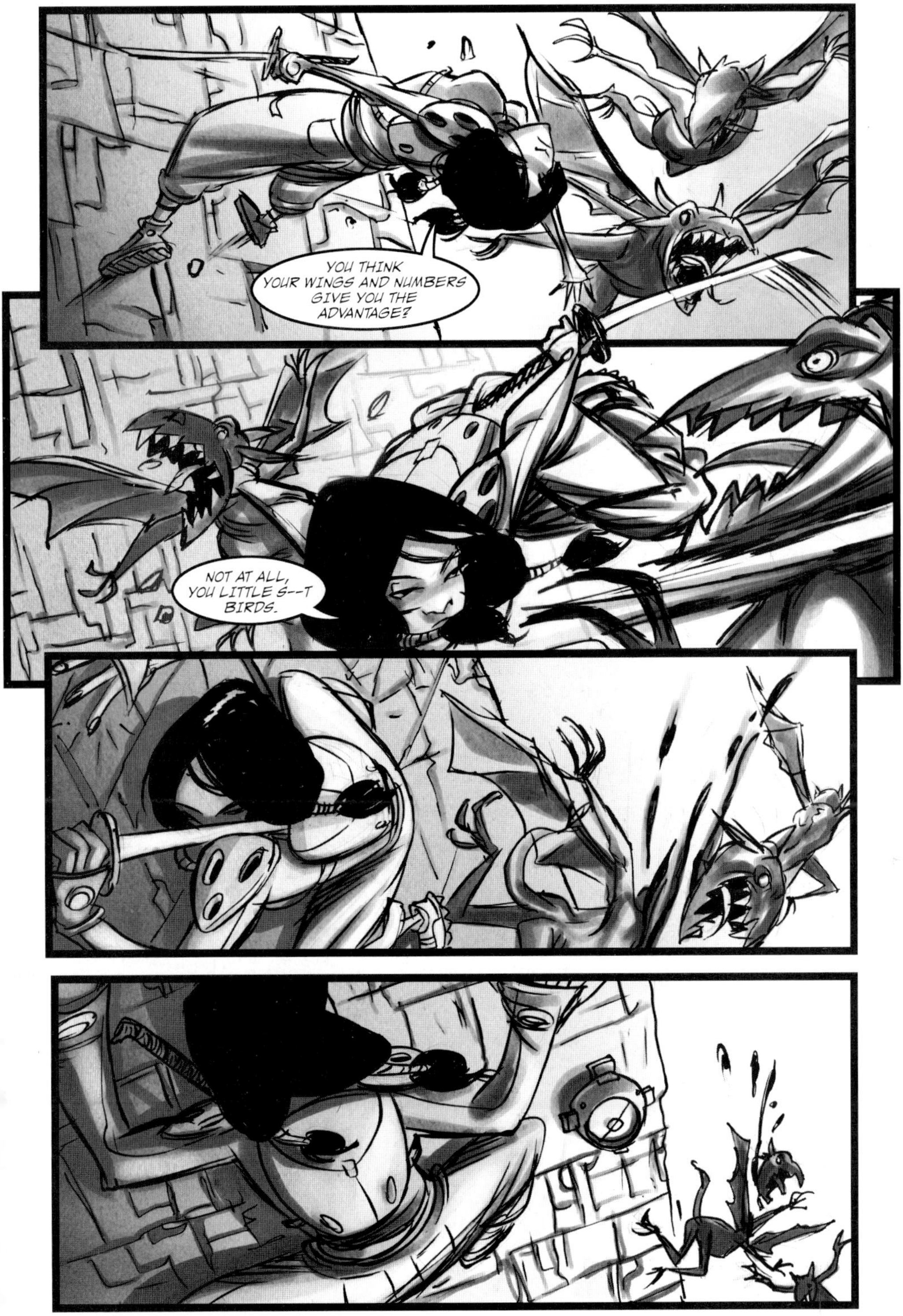
YOU THINK YOUR WINGS AND NUMBERS GIVE YOU THE ADVANTAGE?
NOT AT ALL, YOU LITTLE S--T BIRDS.

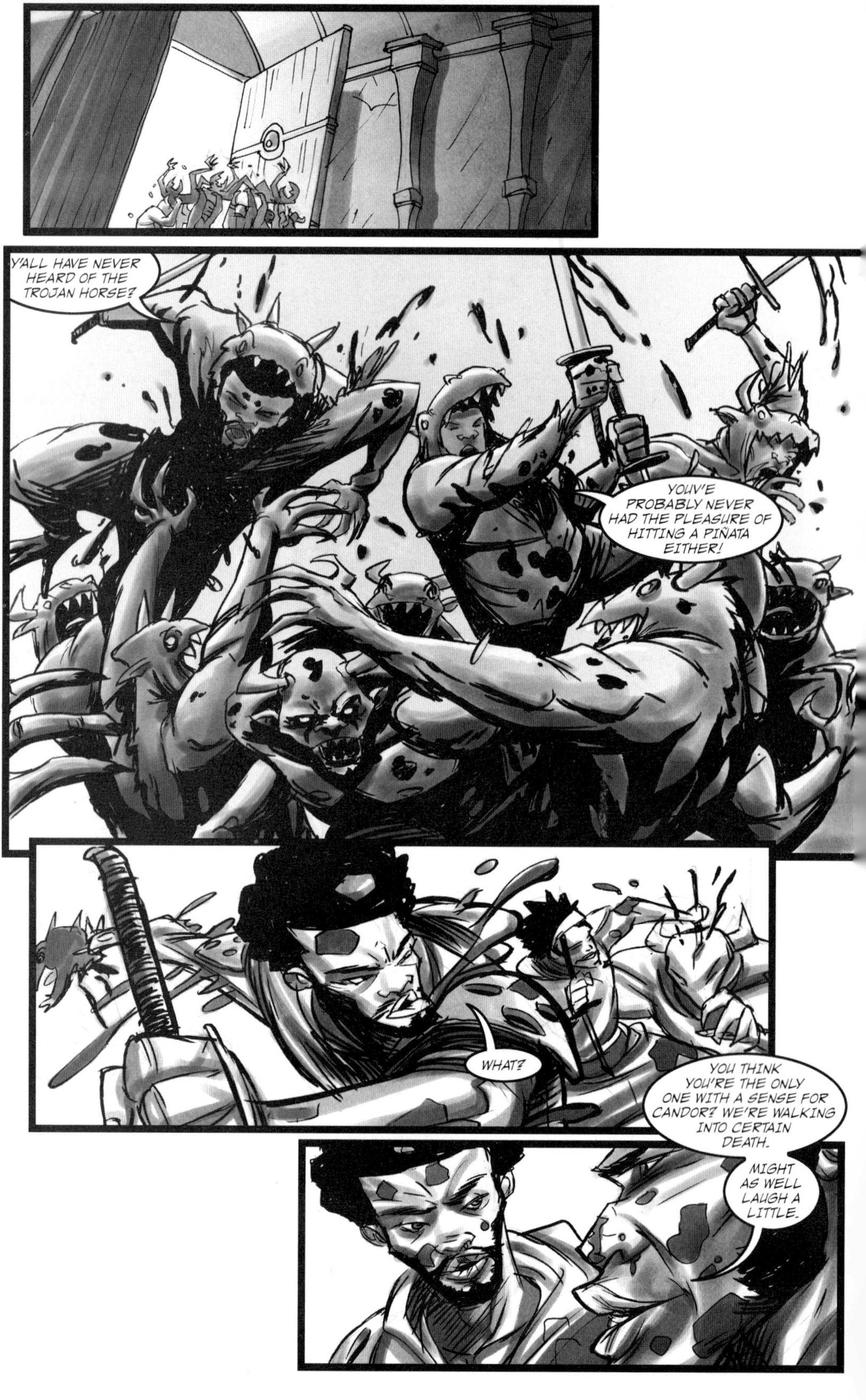

Y'ALL HAVE NEVER HEARD OF THE TROJAN HORSE?
YOUV'E PROBABLY NEVER HAD THE PLEASURE OF HITTING A PIÑATA EITHER!
WHAT?
YOU THINK YOU'RE THE ONLY ONE WITH A SENSE FOR CANDOR? WE'RE WALKING INTO CERTAIN DEATH.
MIGHT AS WELL LAUGH A LITTLE.

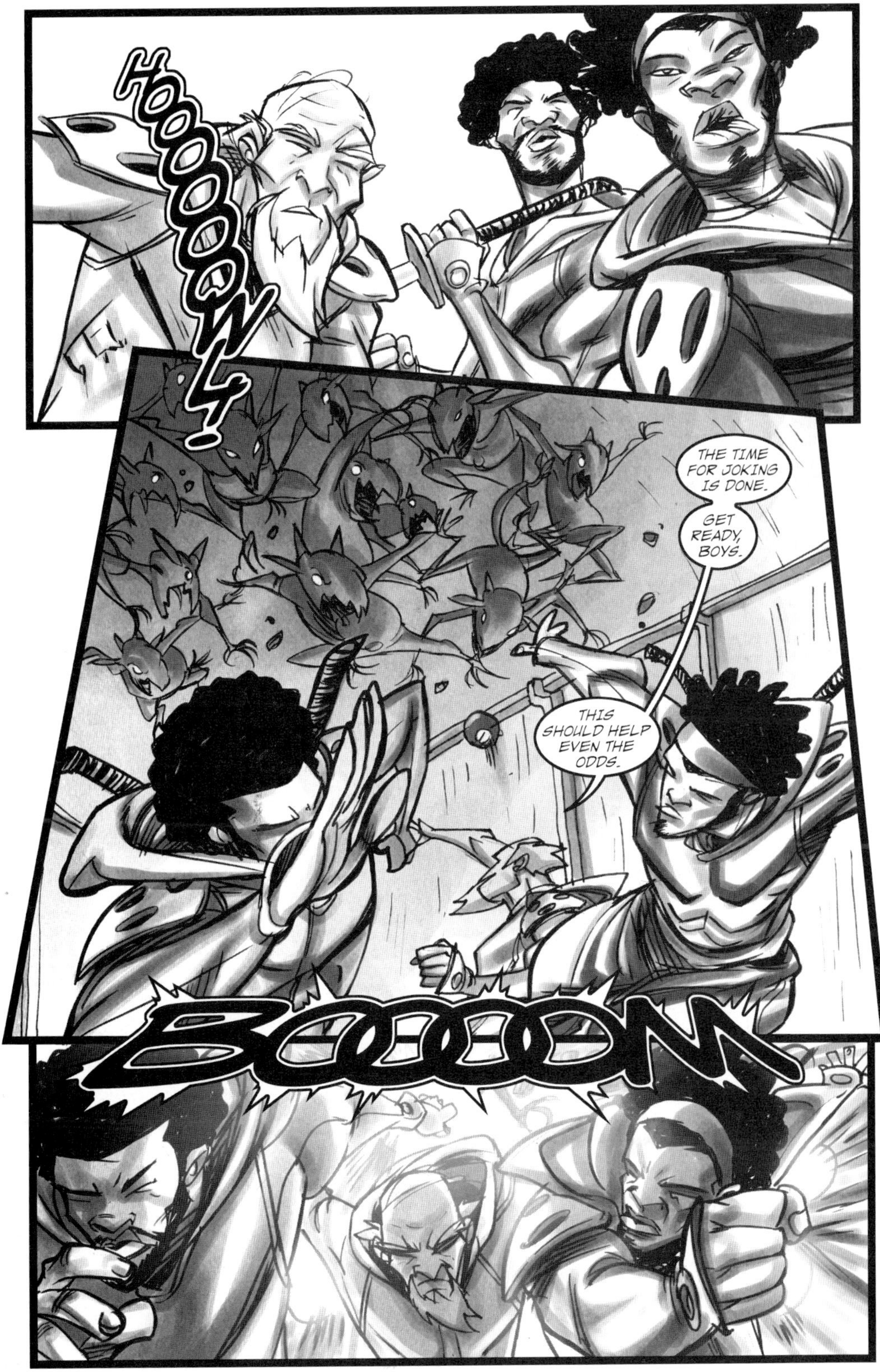
HOOOOOWL!
THE TIME FOR JOKING IS DONE.
GET READY, BOYS.
THIS SHOULD HELP EVEN THE ODDS.
BOOOOM

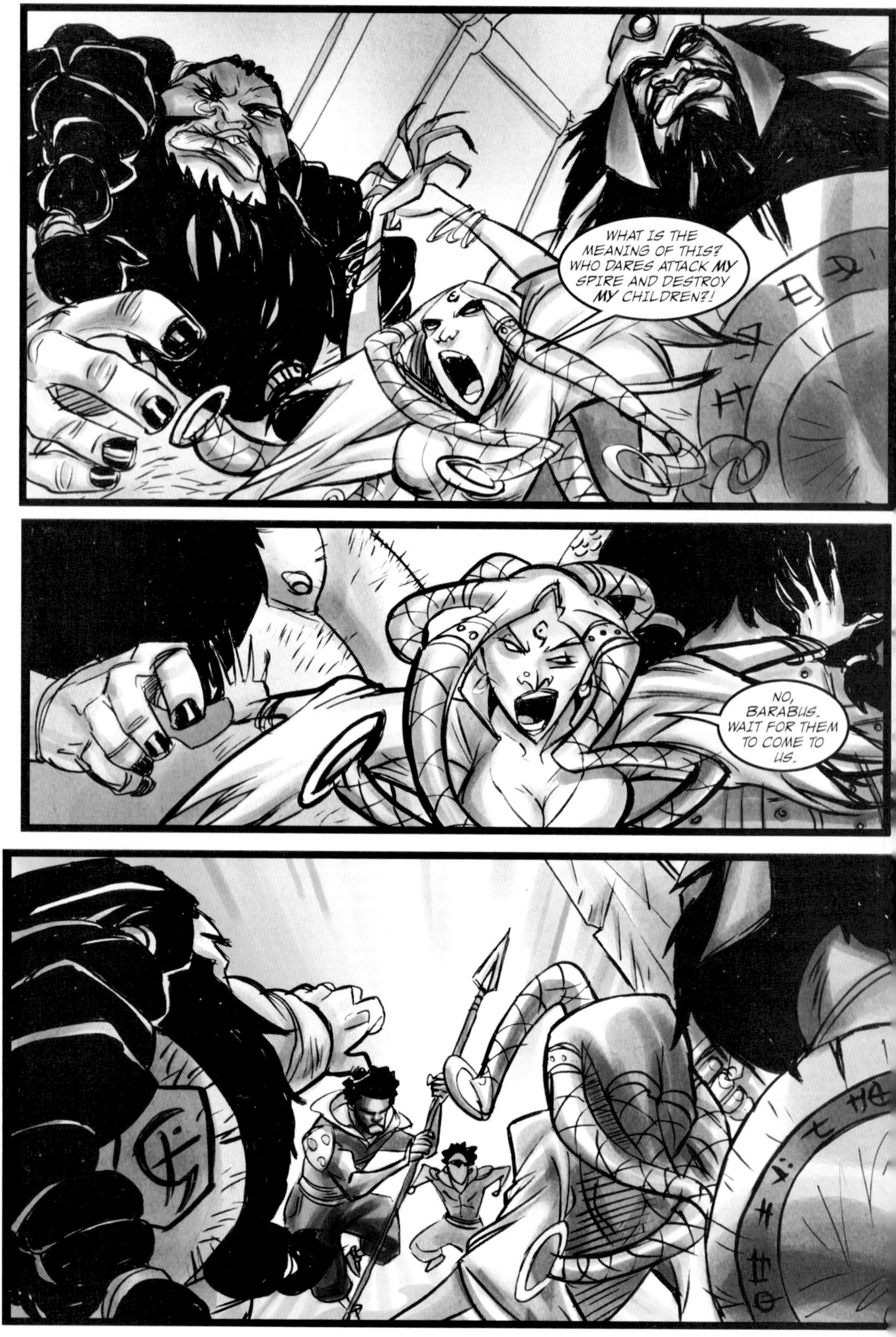
WHAT IS THE MEANING OF THIS? WHO DARES ATTACK MY SPIRE AND DESTROY MY CHILDREN?!
NO, BARABUS. WAIT FOR THEM TO COME TO US.

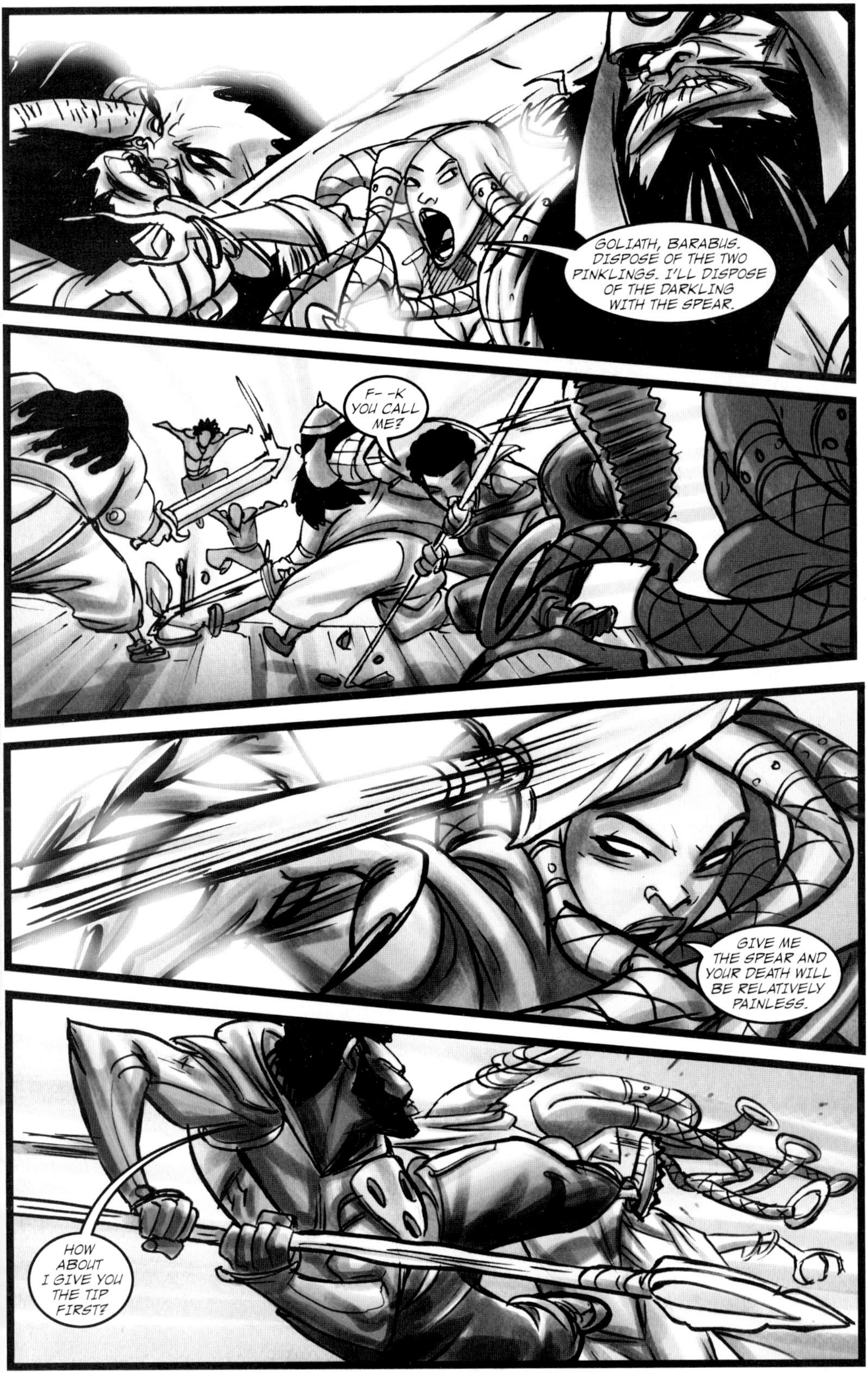
GOLIATH, BARABUS. DISPOSE OF THE TWO PINKLINGS. I'LL DISPOSE OF THE DARKLING WITH THE SPEAR.
F- -K YOU CALL ME?
GIVE ME THE SPEAR AND YOUR DEATH WILL BE RELATIVELY PAINLESS.
HOW ABOUT I GIVE YOU THE TIP FIRST?

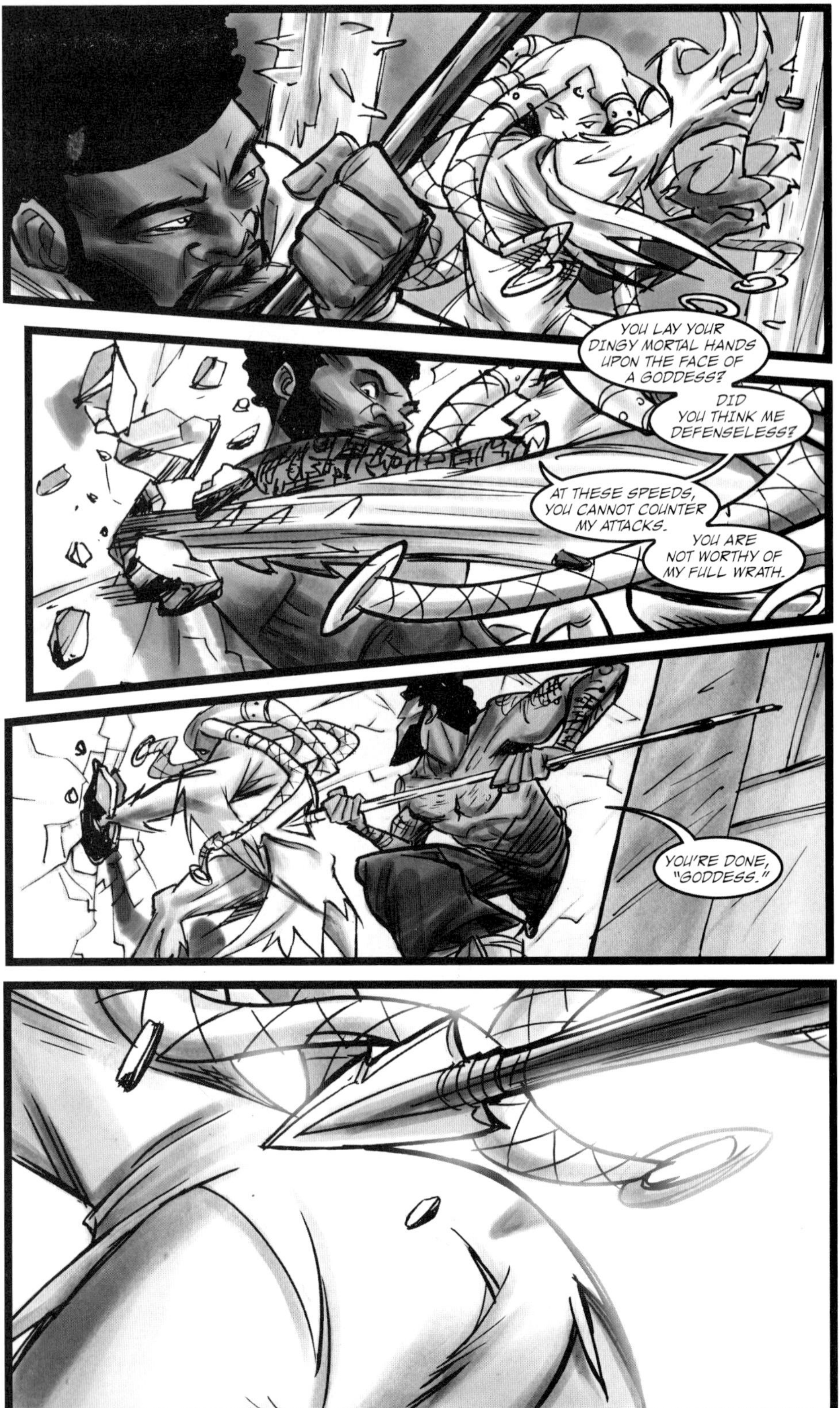
YOU LAY YOUR DINGY MORTAL HANDS UPON THE FACE OF A GODDESS?
DID YOU THINK ME DEFENSELESS?
AT THESE SPEEDS, YOU CANNOT COUNTER MY ATTACKS.
YOU ARE NOT WORTHY OF MY FULL WRATH.
YOU'RE DONE, "GODDESS."

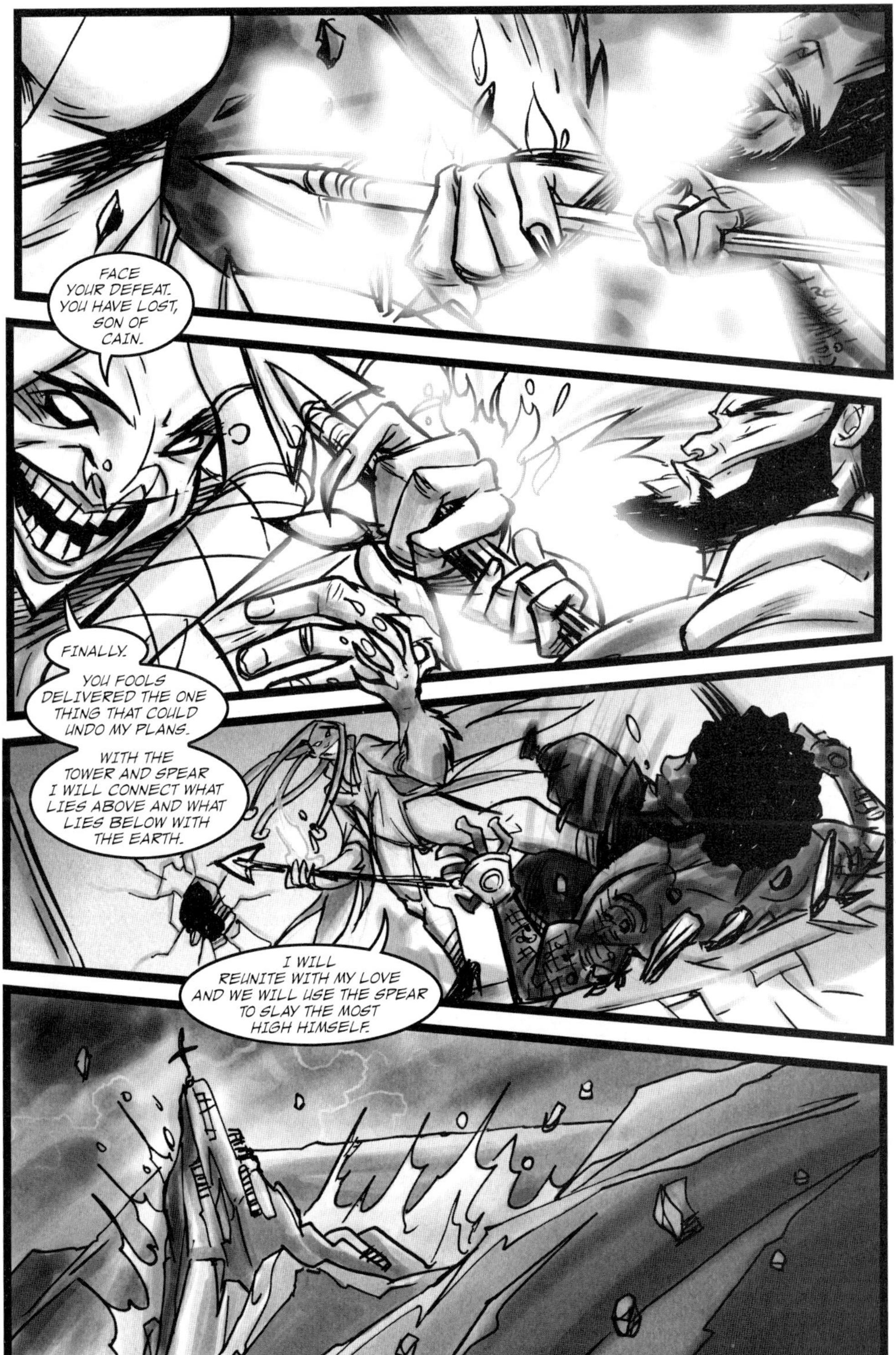
FACE YOUR DEFEAT. YOU HAVE LOST, SON OF CAIN.
FINALLY.
YOU FOOLS DELIVERED THE ONE THING THAT COULD UNDO MY PLANS.
WITH THE TOWER AND SPEAR I WILL CONNECT WHAT LIES ABOVE AND WHAT LIES BELOW WITH THE EARTH.
I WILL REUNITE WITH MY LOVE AND WE WILL USE THE SPEAR TO SLAY THE MOST HIGH HIMSELF.

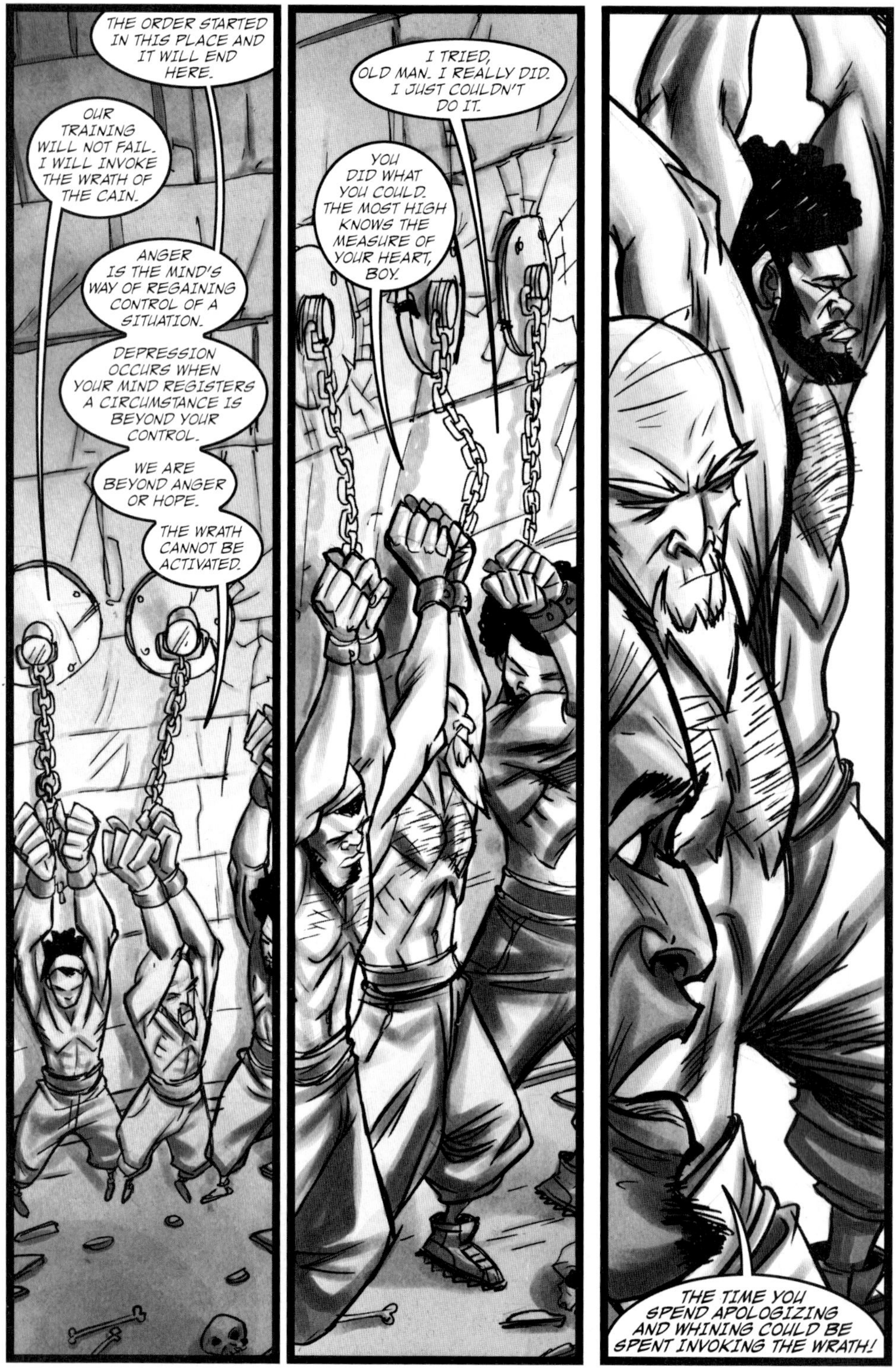
THE ORDER STARTED IN THIS PLACE AND IT WILL END HERE.
OUR TRAINING WILL NOT FAIL. I WILL INVOKE THE WRATH OF THE CAIN.
ANGER IS THE MIND'S WAY OF REGAINING CONTROL OF A SITUATION.
DEPRESSION OCCURS WHEN YOUR MIND REGISTERS A CIRCUMSTANCE IS BEYOND YOUR CONTROL.
WE ARE BEYOND ANGER OR HOPE.
THE WRATH CANNOT BE ACTIVATED.
I TRIED, OLD MAN. I REALLY DID. I JUST COULDN'T DO IT.
YOU DID WHAT YOU COULD. THE MOST HIGH KNOWS THE MEASURE OF YOUR HEART, BOY.
THE TIME YOU SPEND APOLOGIZING AND WHINING COULD BE SPENT INVOKING THE WRATH!

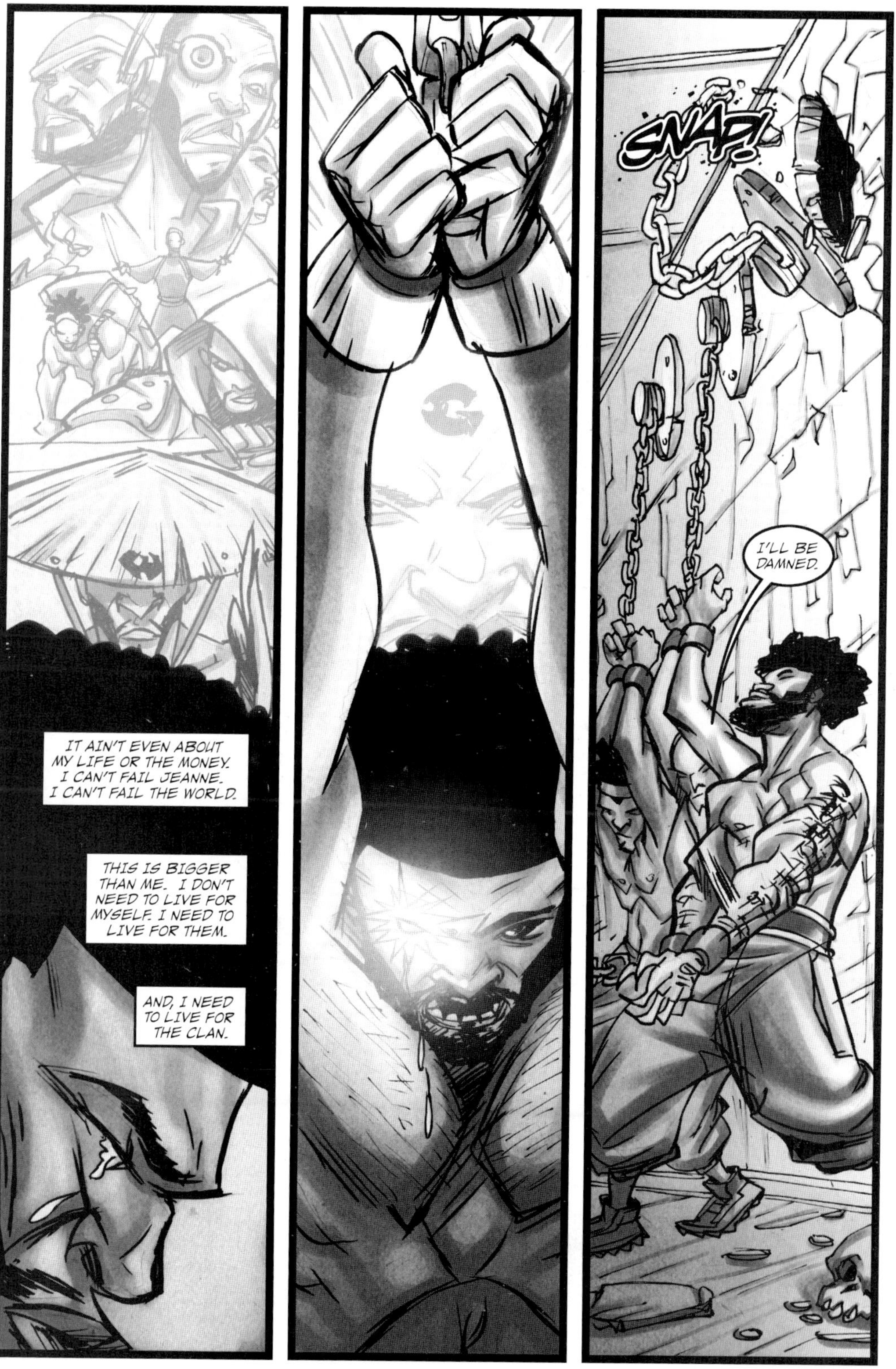

IT AIN'T EVEN ABOUT MY LIFE OR THE MONEY. I CAN'T FAIL JEANNE. I CAN'T FAIL THE WORLD.
THIS IS BIGGER THAN ME. I DON'T NEED TO LIVE FOR MYSELF. I NEED TO LIVE FOR THEM.
AND, I NEED TO LIVE FOR THE CLAN.
SNAP!
I'LL BE DAMNED.

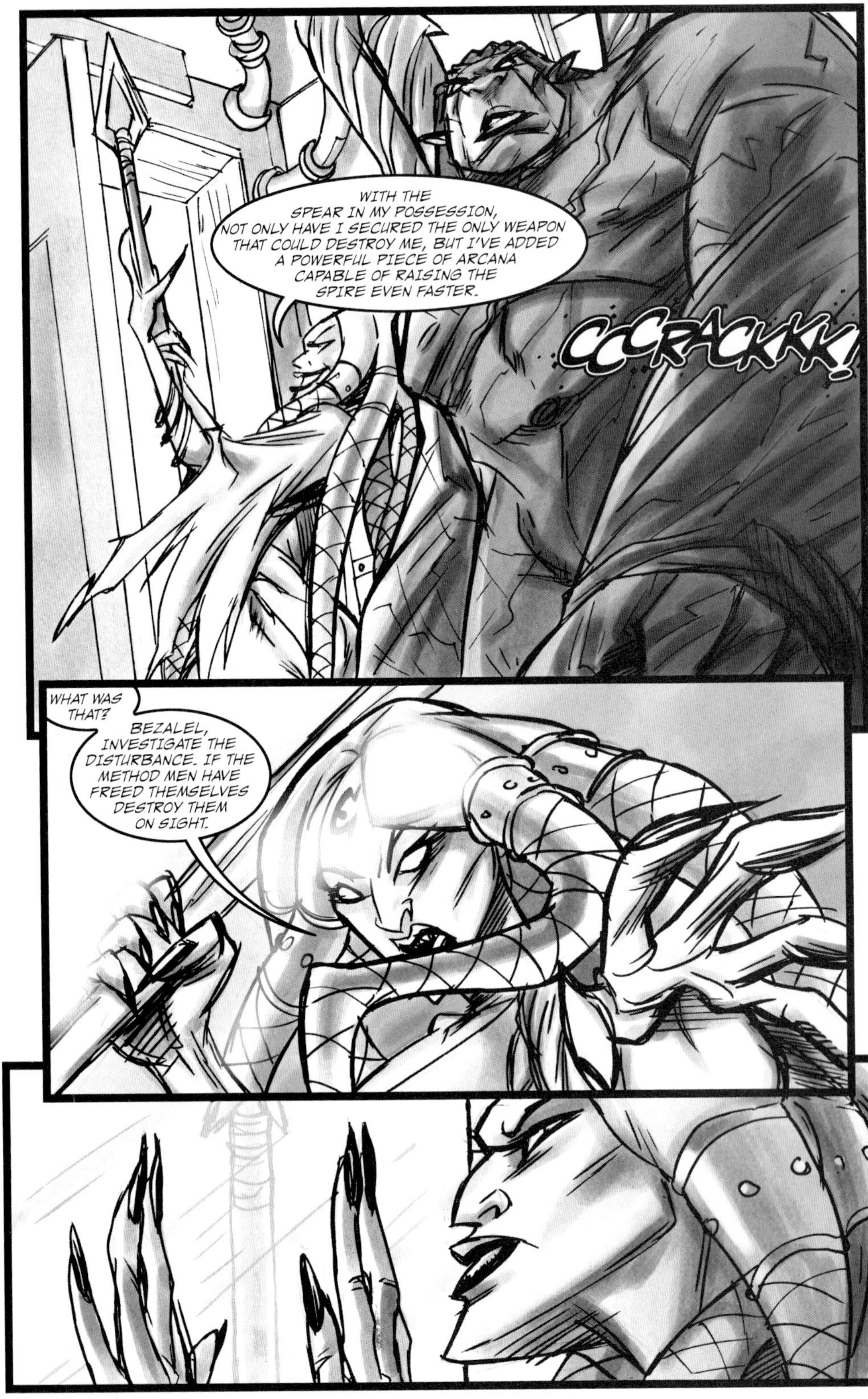
WITH THE SPEAR IN MY POSSESSION, NOT ONLY HAVE I SECURED THE ONLY WEAPON THAT COULD DESTROY ME, BUT I'VE ADDED A POWERFUL PIECE OF ARCANA CAPABLE OF RAISING THE SPIRE EVEN FASTER.
CCCRACKKKK!
WHAT WAS THAT?
BEZALEL, INVESTIGATE THE DISTURBANCE. IF THE METHOD MEN HAVE FREED THEMSELVES DESTROY THEM ON SIGHT.

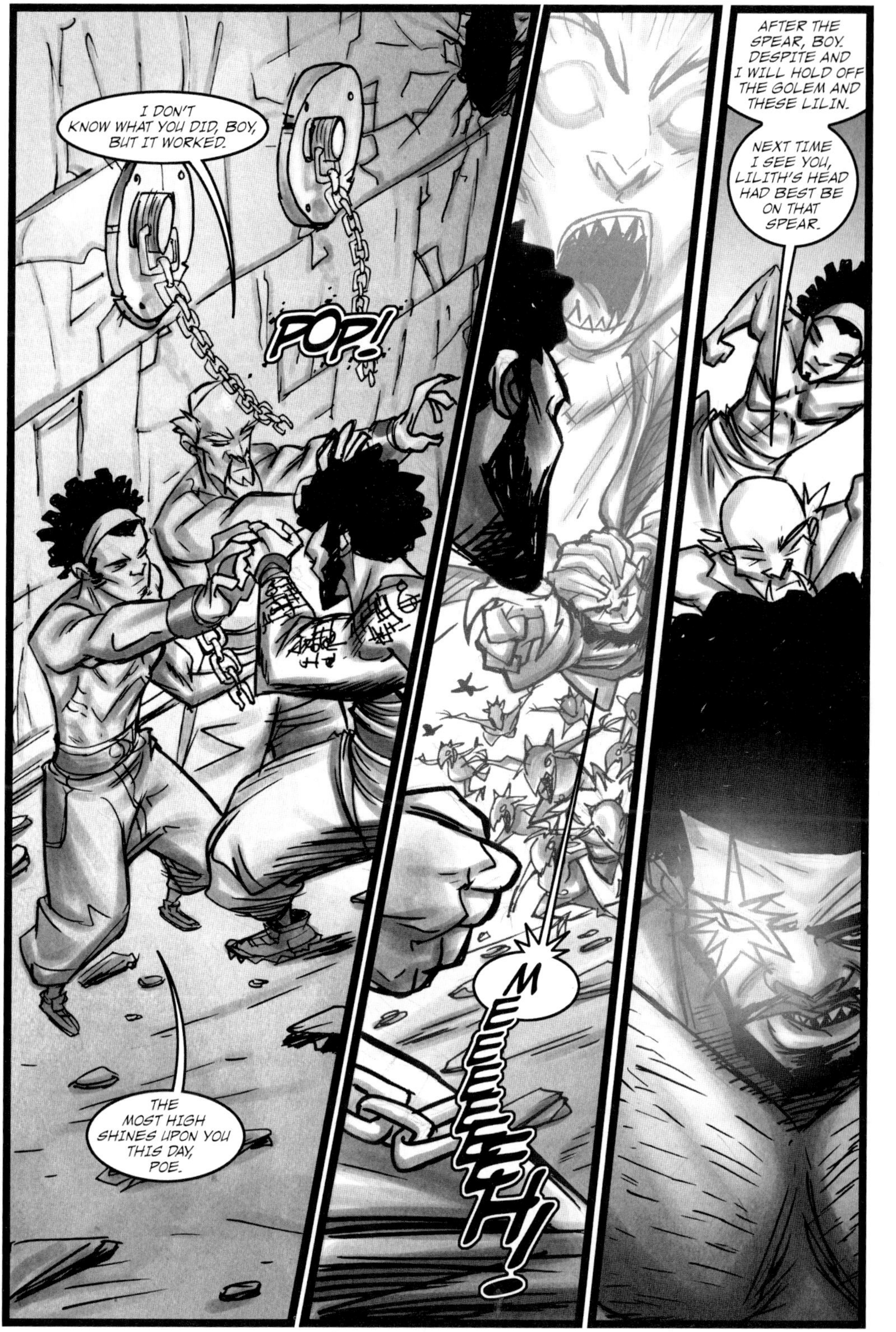
I DON'T KNOW WHAT YOU DID, BOY, BUT IT WORKED.
POP!
THE MOST HIGH SHINES UPON YOU THIS DAY, POE.
MEEEEEEECH!
AFTER THE SPEAR, BOY. DESPITE AND I WILL HOLD OFF THE GOLEM AND THESE LILIN.
NEXT TIME I SEE YOU, LILITH'S HEAD HAD BEST BE ON THAT SPEAR.

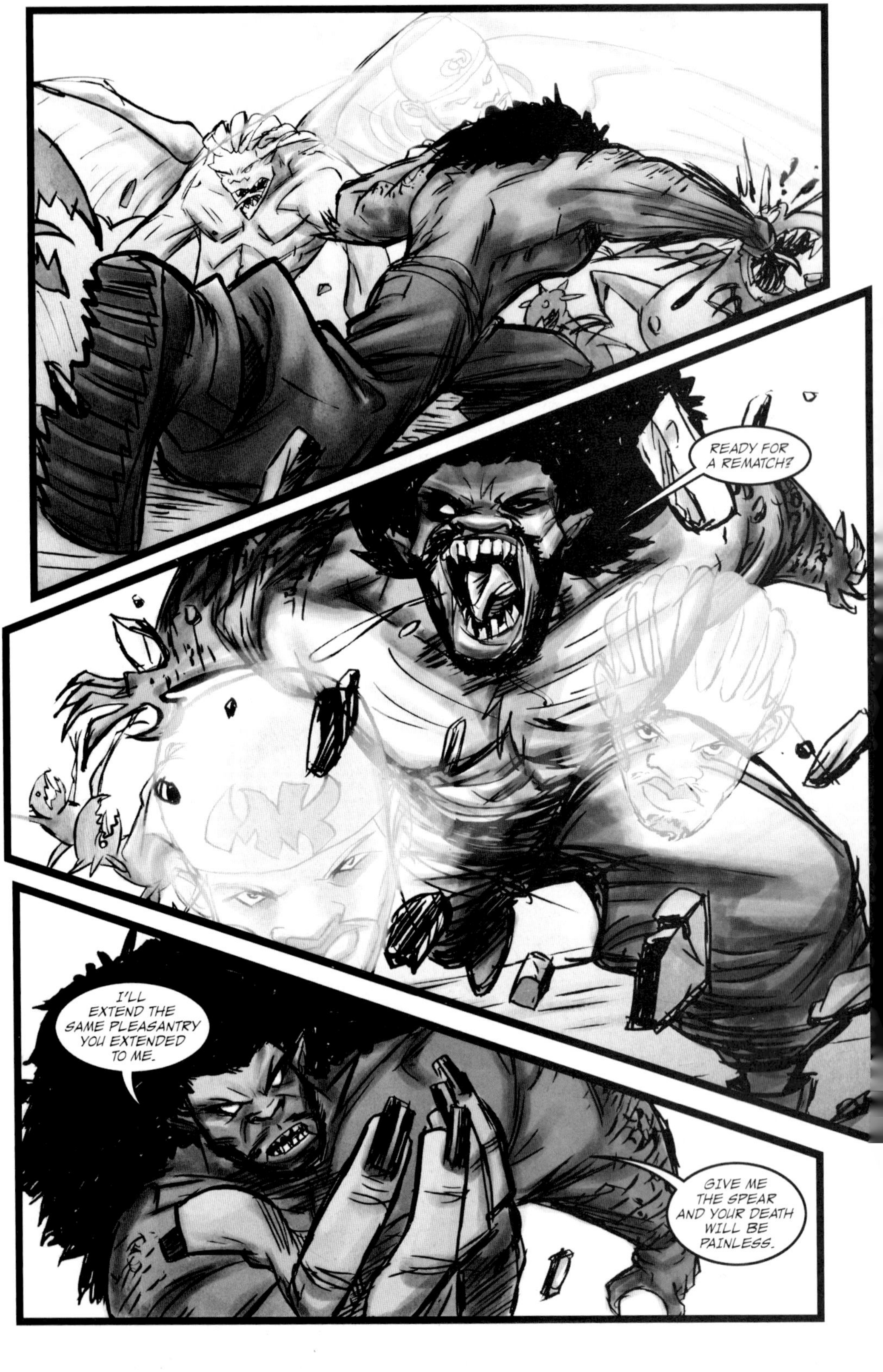
READY FOR A REMATCH?
I'LL EXTEND THE SAME PLEASANTRY YOU EXTENDED TO ME.
GIVE ME THE SPEAR AND YOUR DEATH WILL BE PAINLESS.

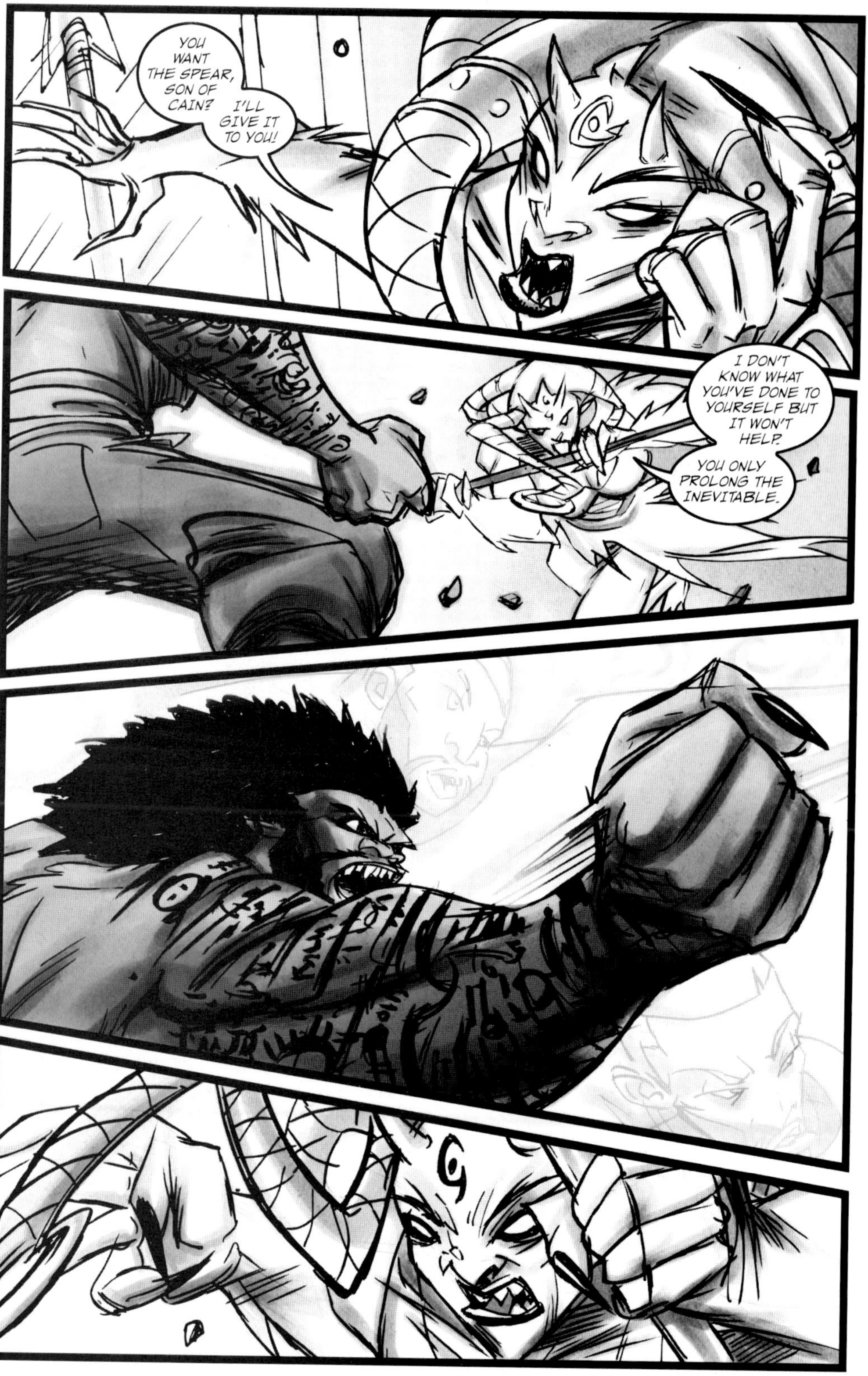
YOU WANT THE SPEAR, SON OF CAIN?
I'LL GIVE IT TO YOU!
I DON'T KNOW WHAT YOU'VE DONE TO YOURSELF BUT IT WON'T HELP.
YOU ONLY PROLONG THE INEVITABLE.

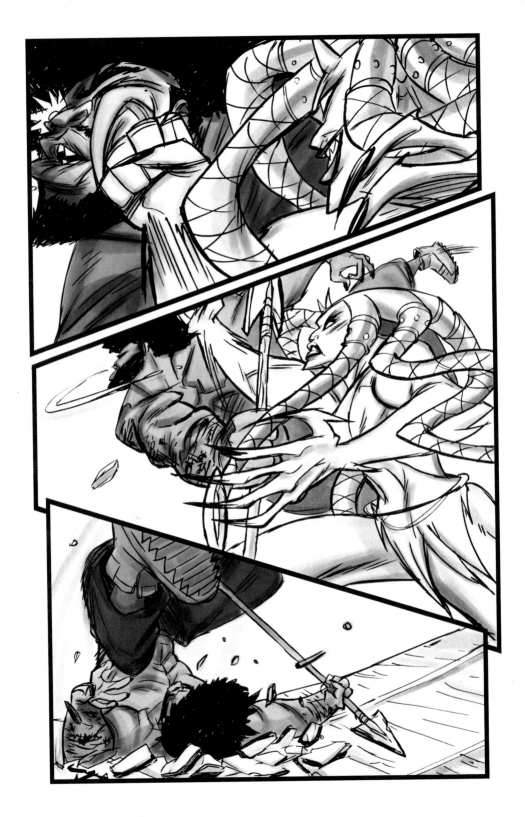

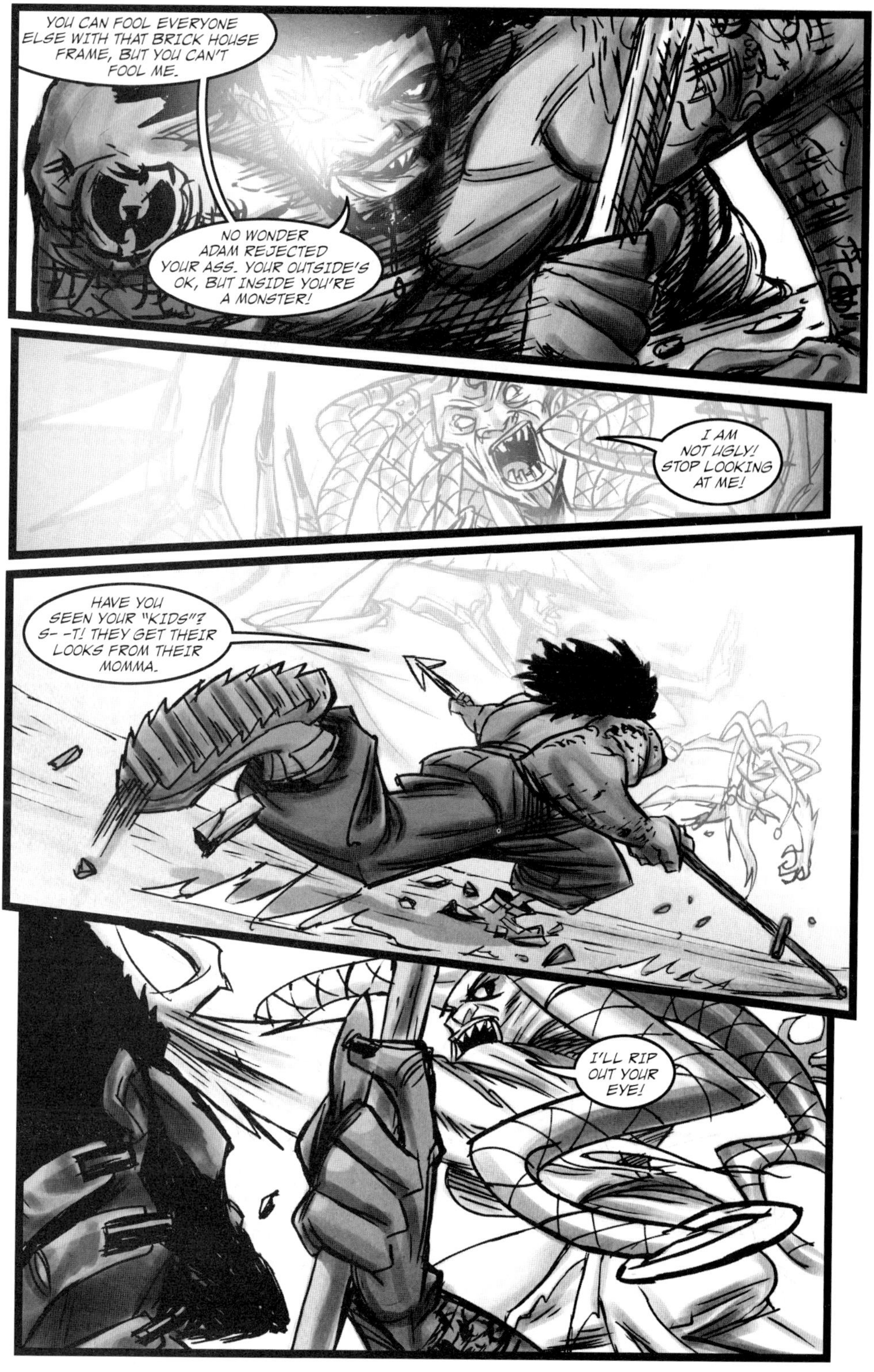
YOU CAN FOOL EVERYONE ELSE WITH THAT BRICK HOUSE FRAME, BUT YOU CAN'T FOOL ME.
NO WONDER ADAM REJECTED YOUR ASS. YOUR OUTSIDE'S OK, BUT INSIDE YOU'RE A MONSTER!
I AM NOT UGLY! STOP LOOKING AT ME!
HAVE YOU SEEN YOUR "KIDS"? S- -T! THEY GET THEIR LOOKS FROM THEIR MOMMA.
I'LL RIP OUT YOUR EYE!

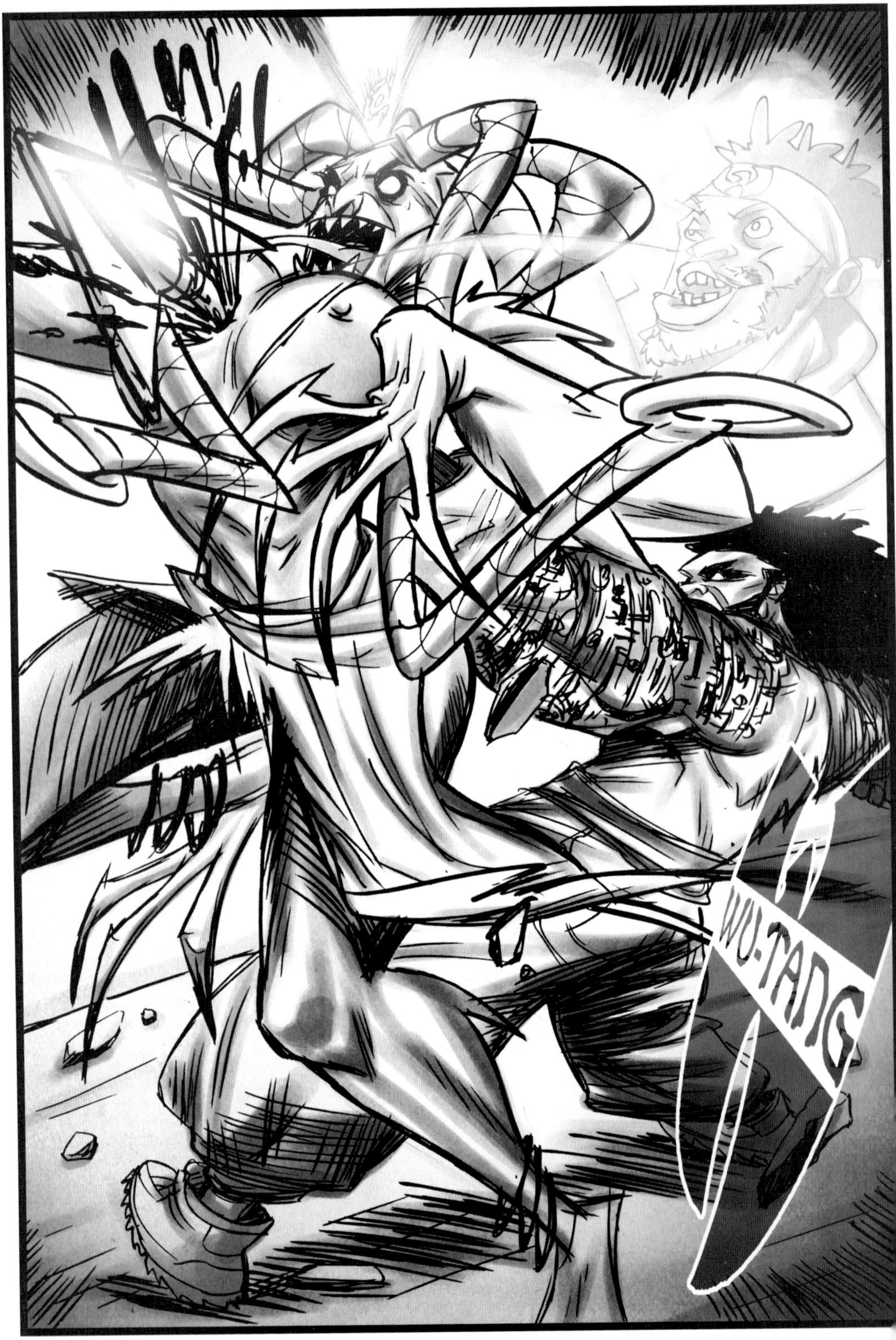
WU-TANG

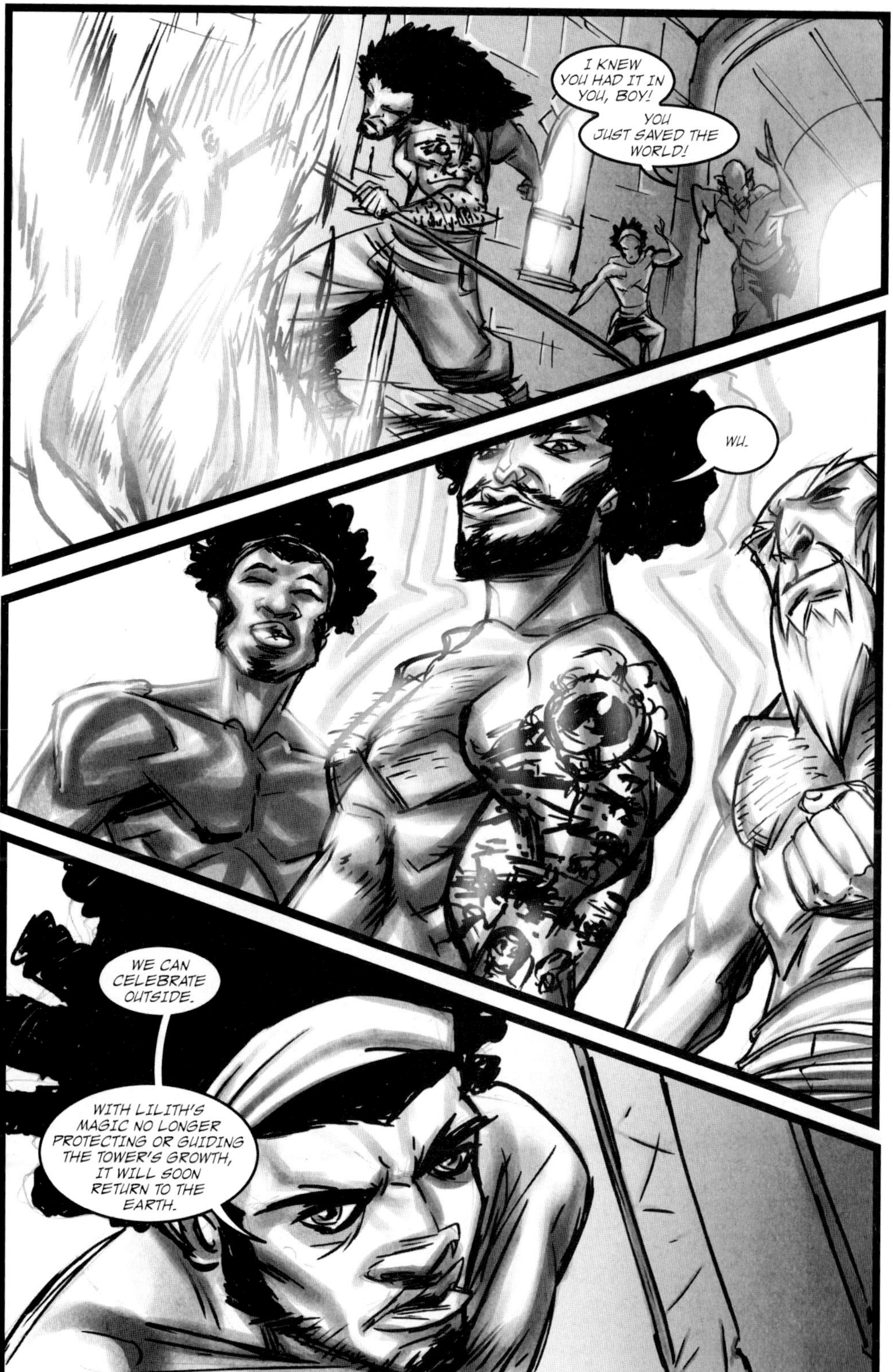
I KNEW YOU HAD IT IN YOU, BOY!
YOU JUST SAVED THE WORLD!
WU.
WE CAN CELEBRATE OUTSIDE.
WITH LILITH'S MAGIC NO LONGER PROTECTING OR GUIDING THE TOWER'S GROWTH, IT WILL SOON RETURN TO THE EARTH.

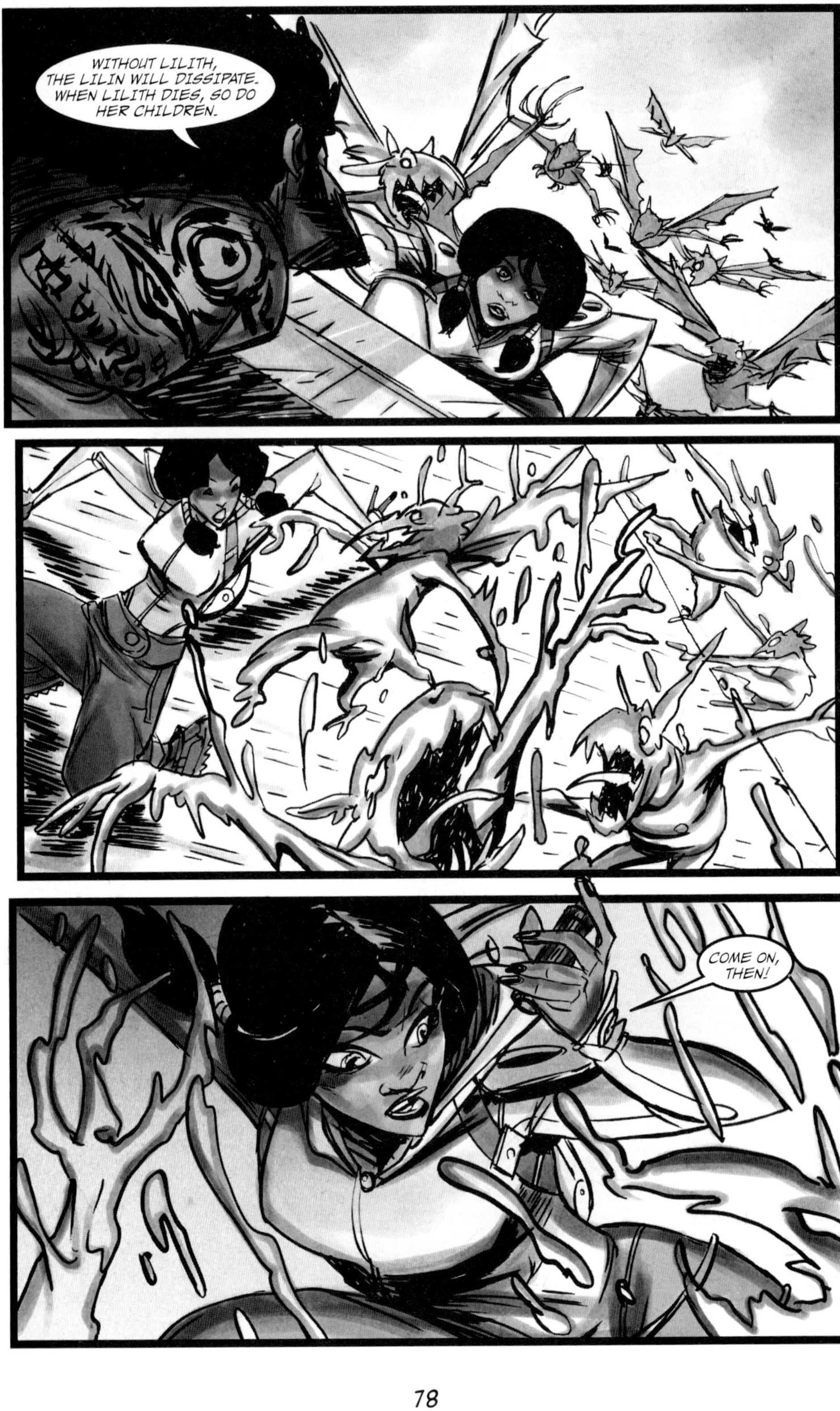
WITHOUT LILITH, THE LILIN WILL DISSIPATE. WHEN LILITH DIES, SO DO HER CHILDREN.
COME ON, THEN!

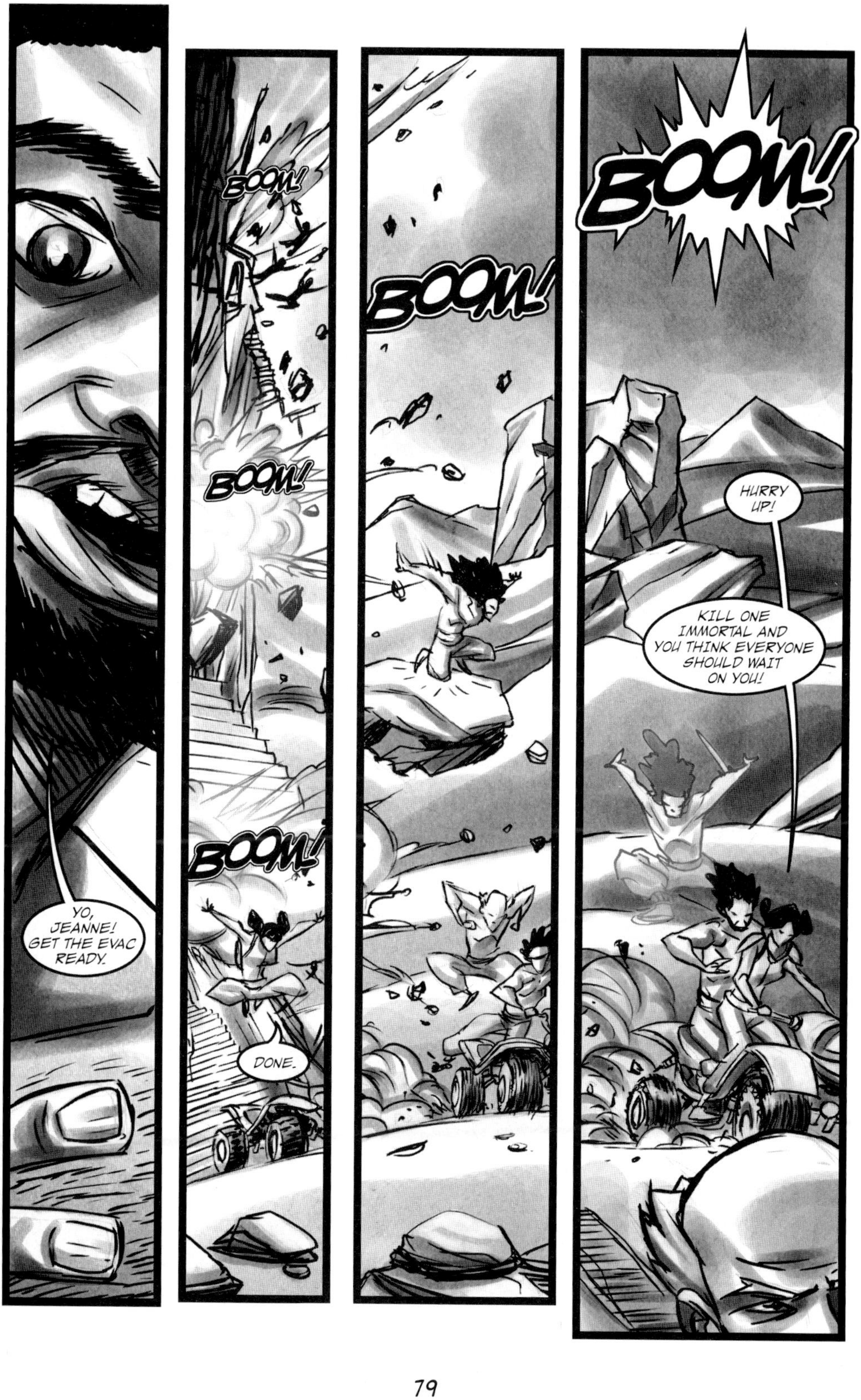
YO, JEANNE! GET THE EVAC READY.
BOOM!
BOOM!
BOOM!
DONE.
BOOM!
BOOM!
HURRY UP!
KILL ONE IMMORTAL AND YOU THINK EVERYONE SHOULD WAIT ON YOU!

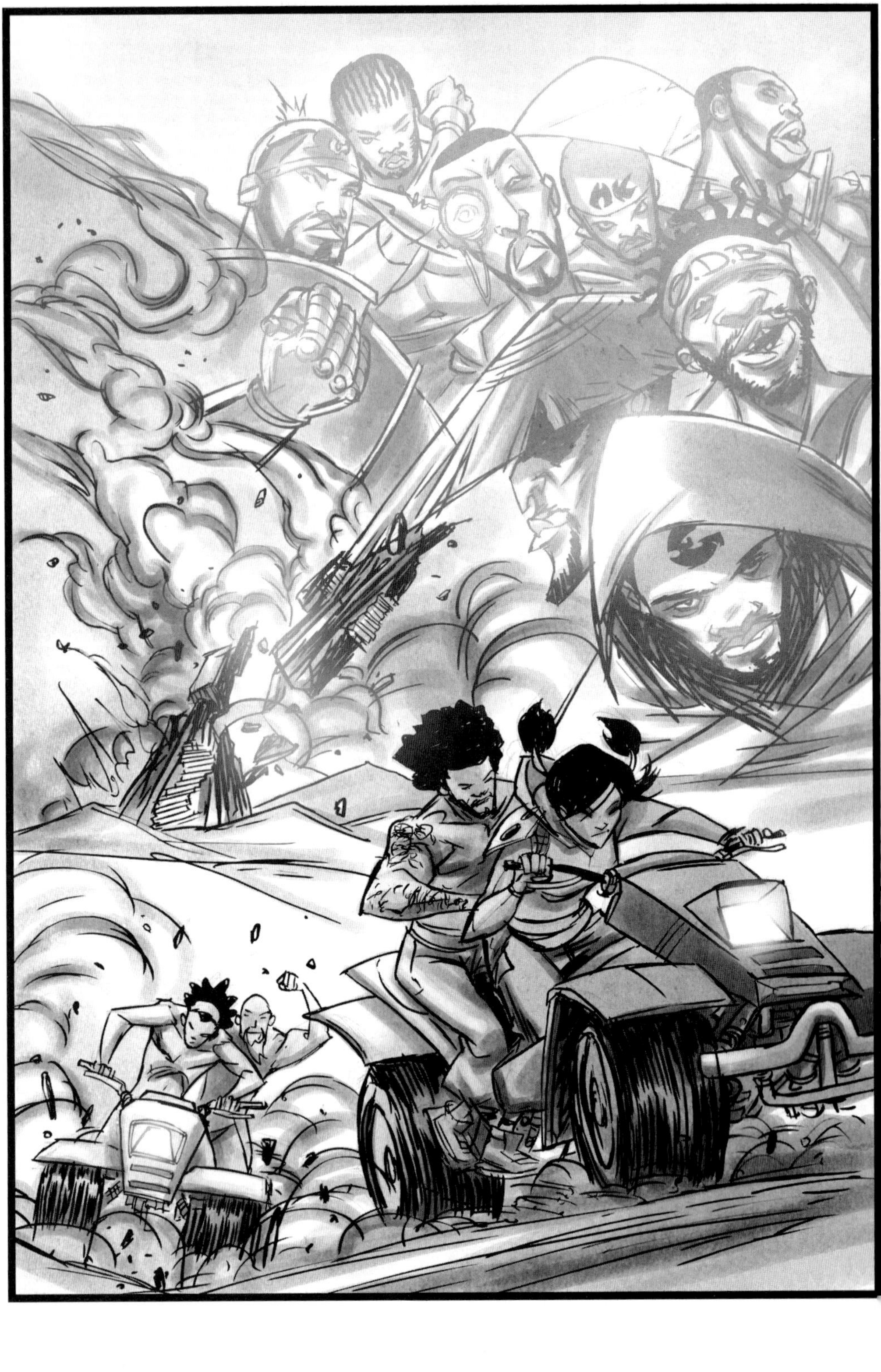

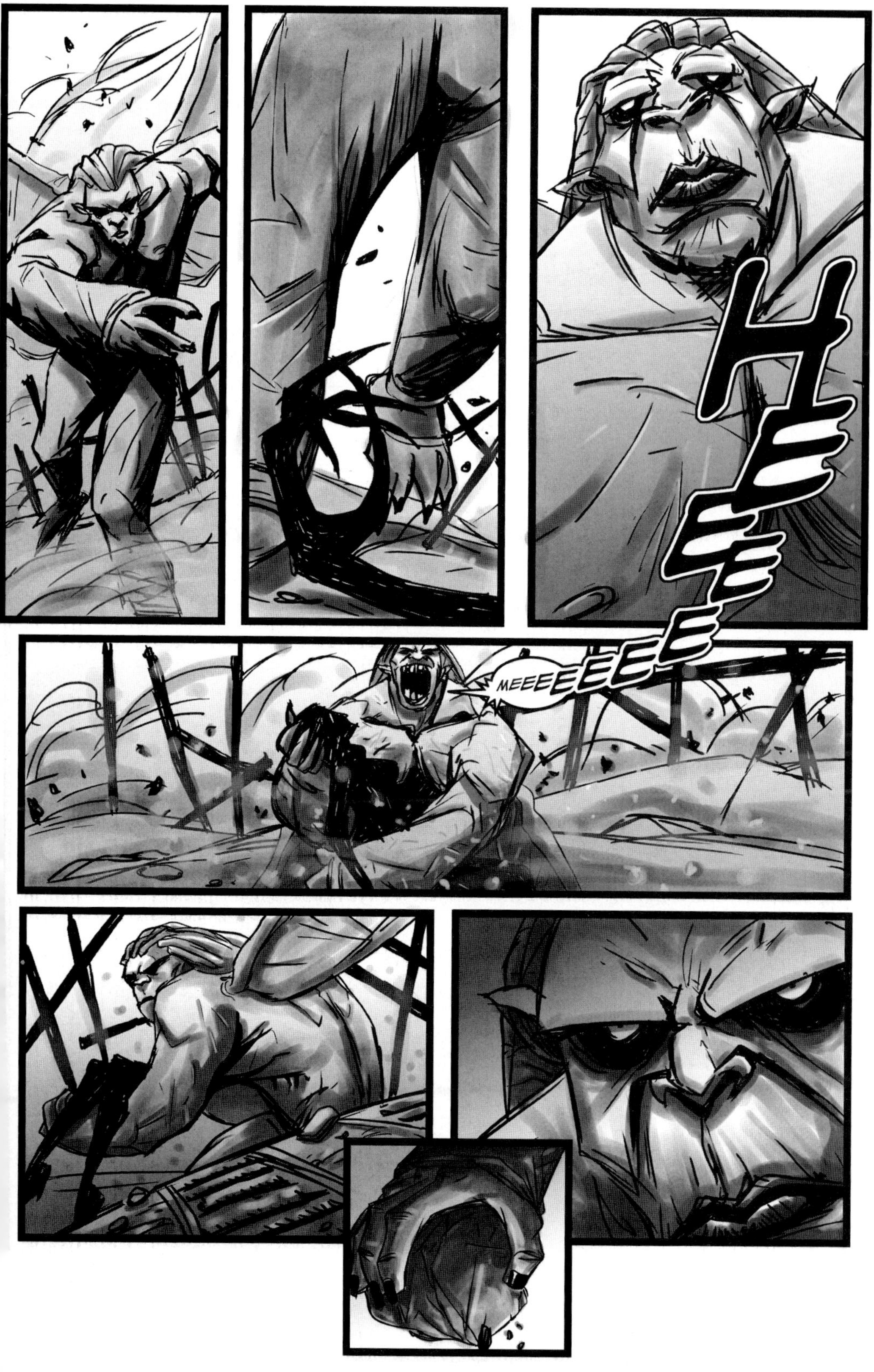
HEEEEEEEEE
MEEEEEEEEEEE

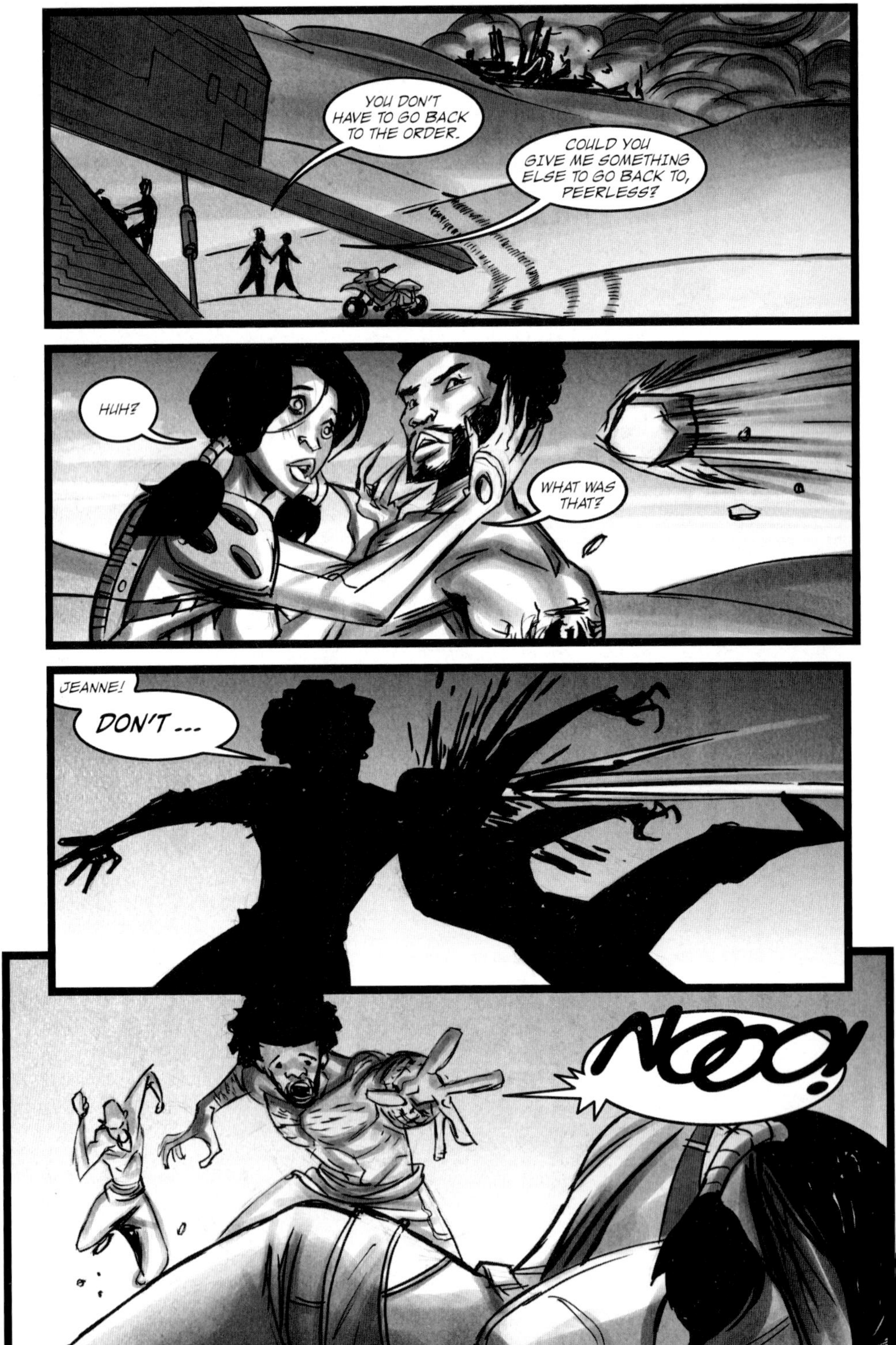
YOU DON'T HAVE TO GO BACK TO THE ORDER.
COULD YOU GIVE ME SOMETHING ELSE TO GO BACK TO, PEERLESS?
HUH?
WHAT WAS THAT?
JEANNE!
DON'T ...
NOOO!

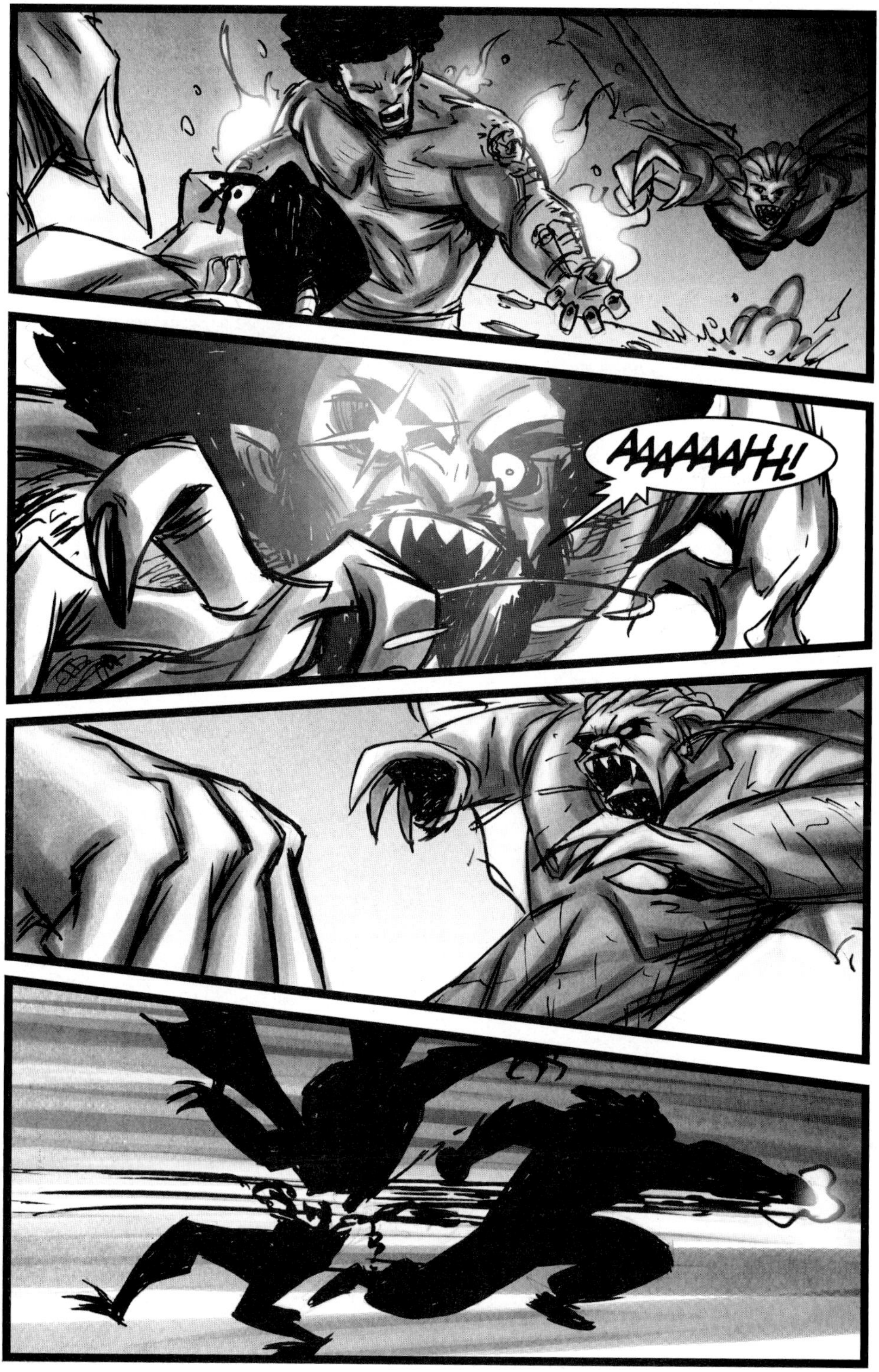
AAAAAAHH!

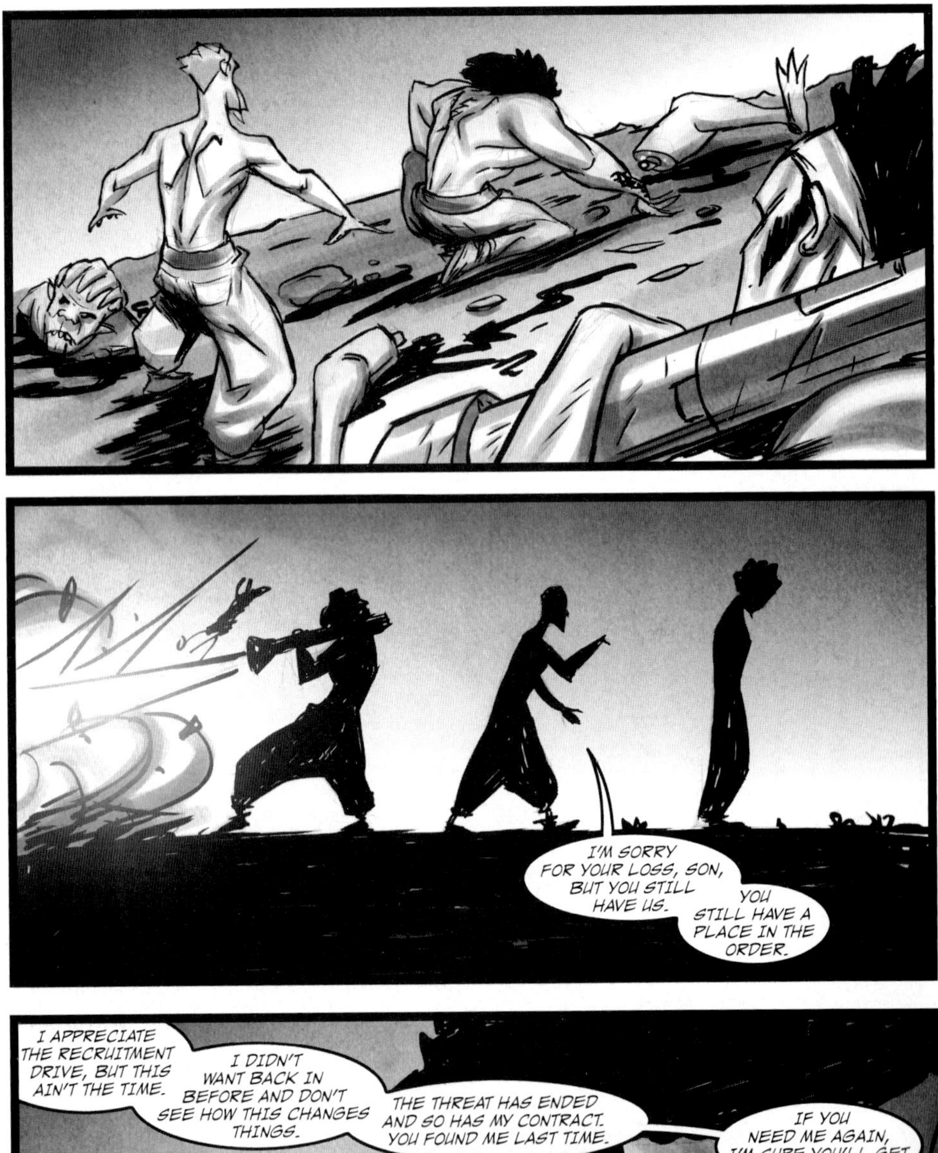
I'M SORRY FOR YOUR LOSS, SON, BUT YOU STILL HAVE US.
YOU STILL HAVE A PLACE IN THE ORDER.
I APPRECIATE THE RECRUITMENT DRIVE, BUT THIS AIN'T THE TIME.
I DIDN'T WANT BACK IN BEFORE AND DON'T SEE HOW THIS CHANGES THINGS.
THE THREAT HAS ENDED AND SO HAS MY CONTRACT. YOU FOUND ME LAST TIME.
IF YOU NEED ME AGAIN, I'M SURE YOU'LL GET AT ME.

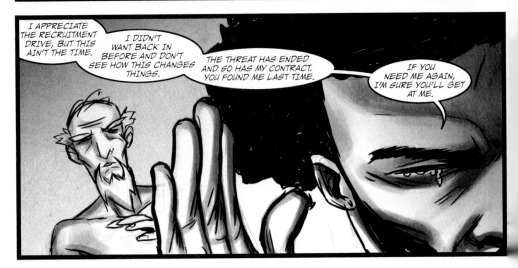

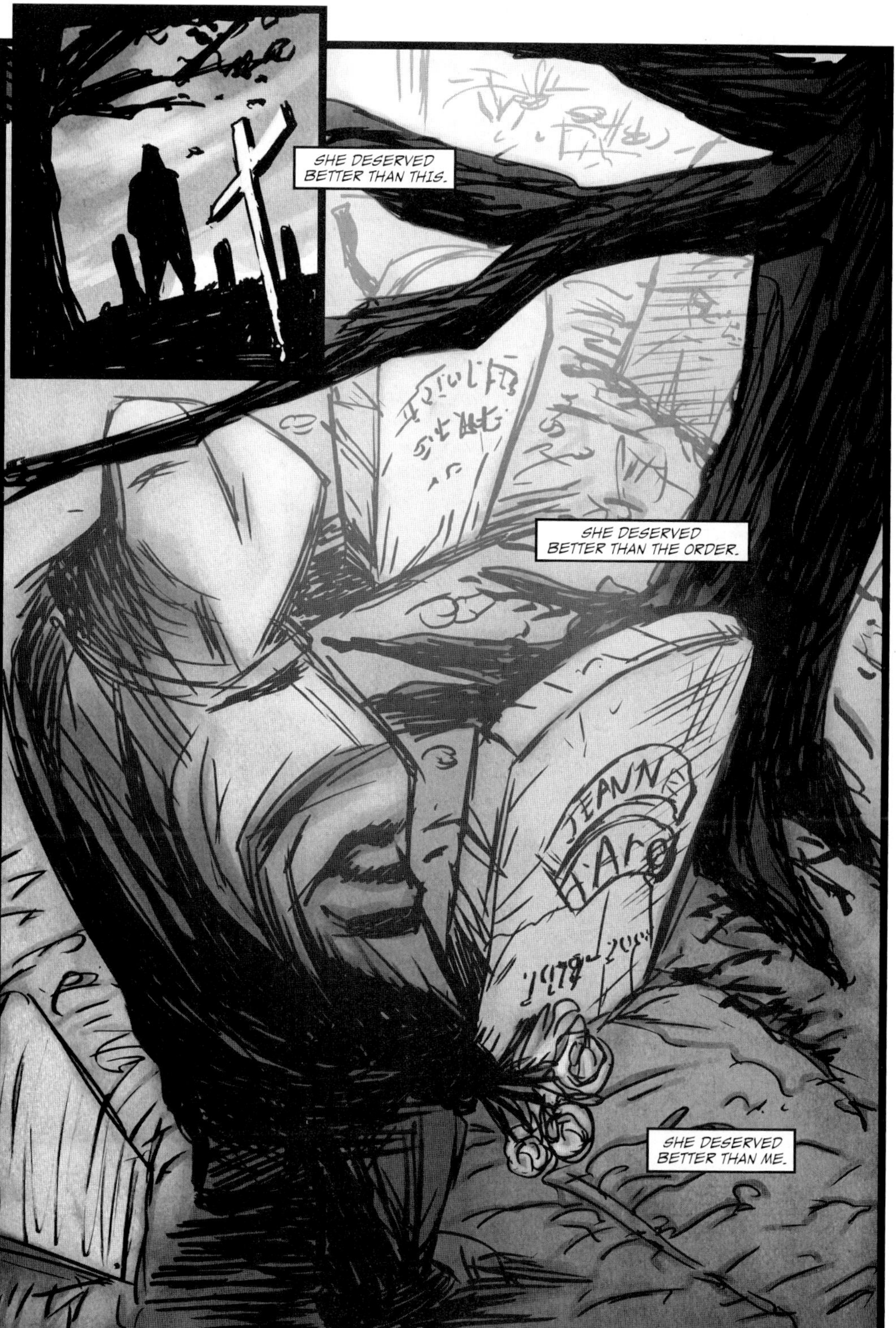
SHE DESERVED BETTER THAN THIS.
SHE DESERVED BETTER THAN THE ORDER.
SHE DESERVED BETTER THAN ME.

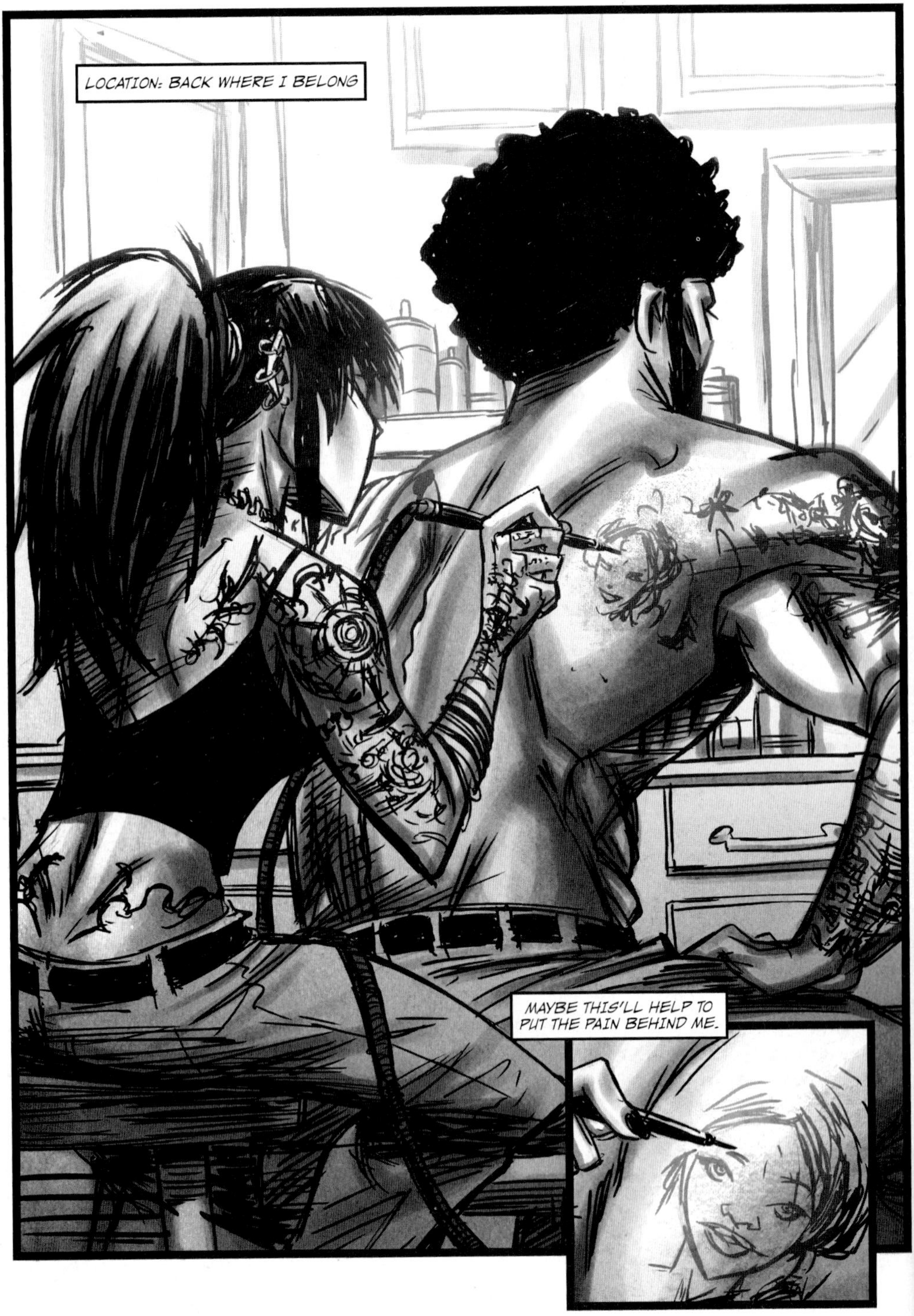
LOCATION: BACK WHERE I BELONG
MAYBE THIS'LL HELP TO PUT THE PAIN BEHIND ME.

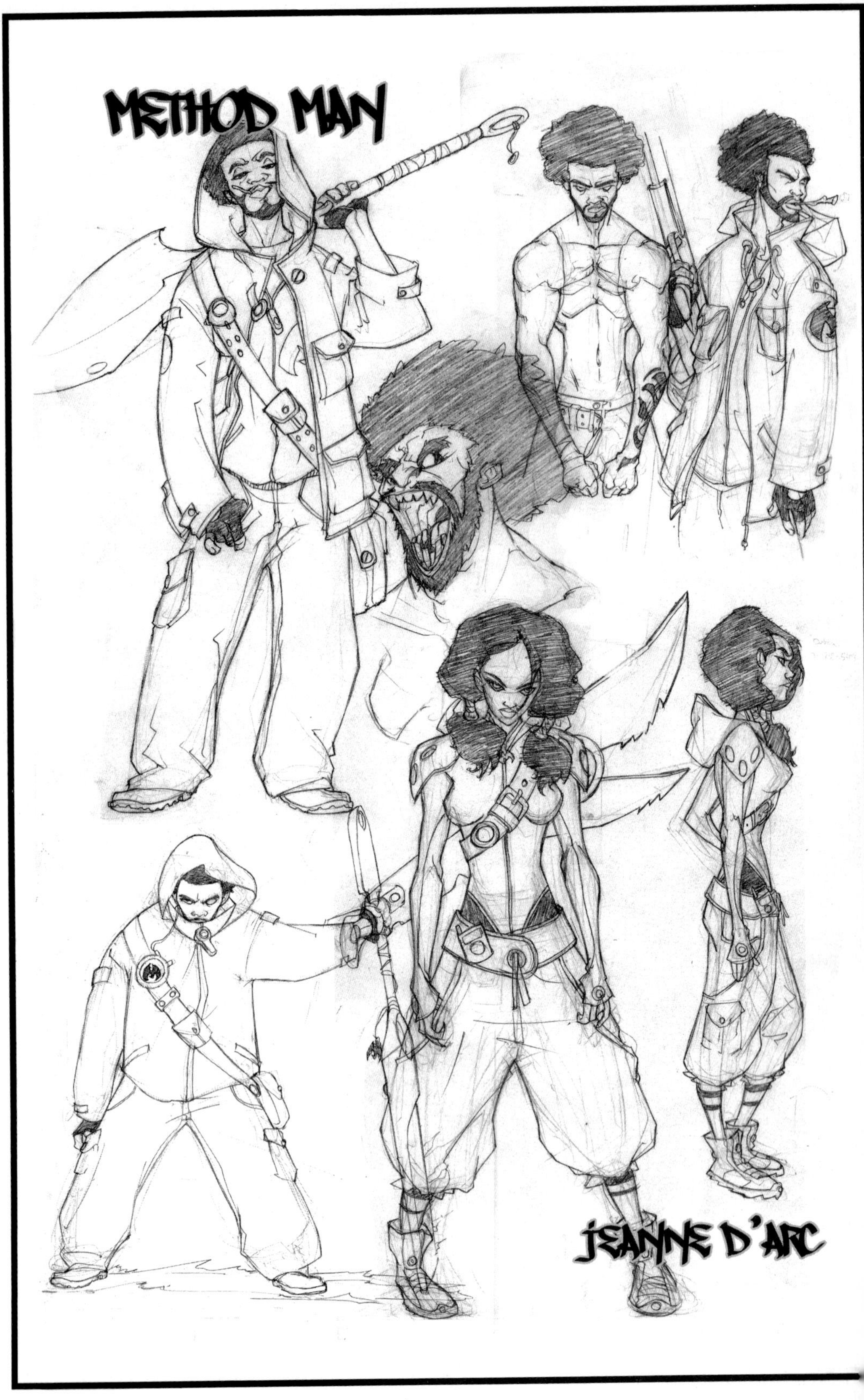
METHOD MAN
JEANNE D'ARC

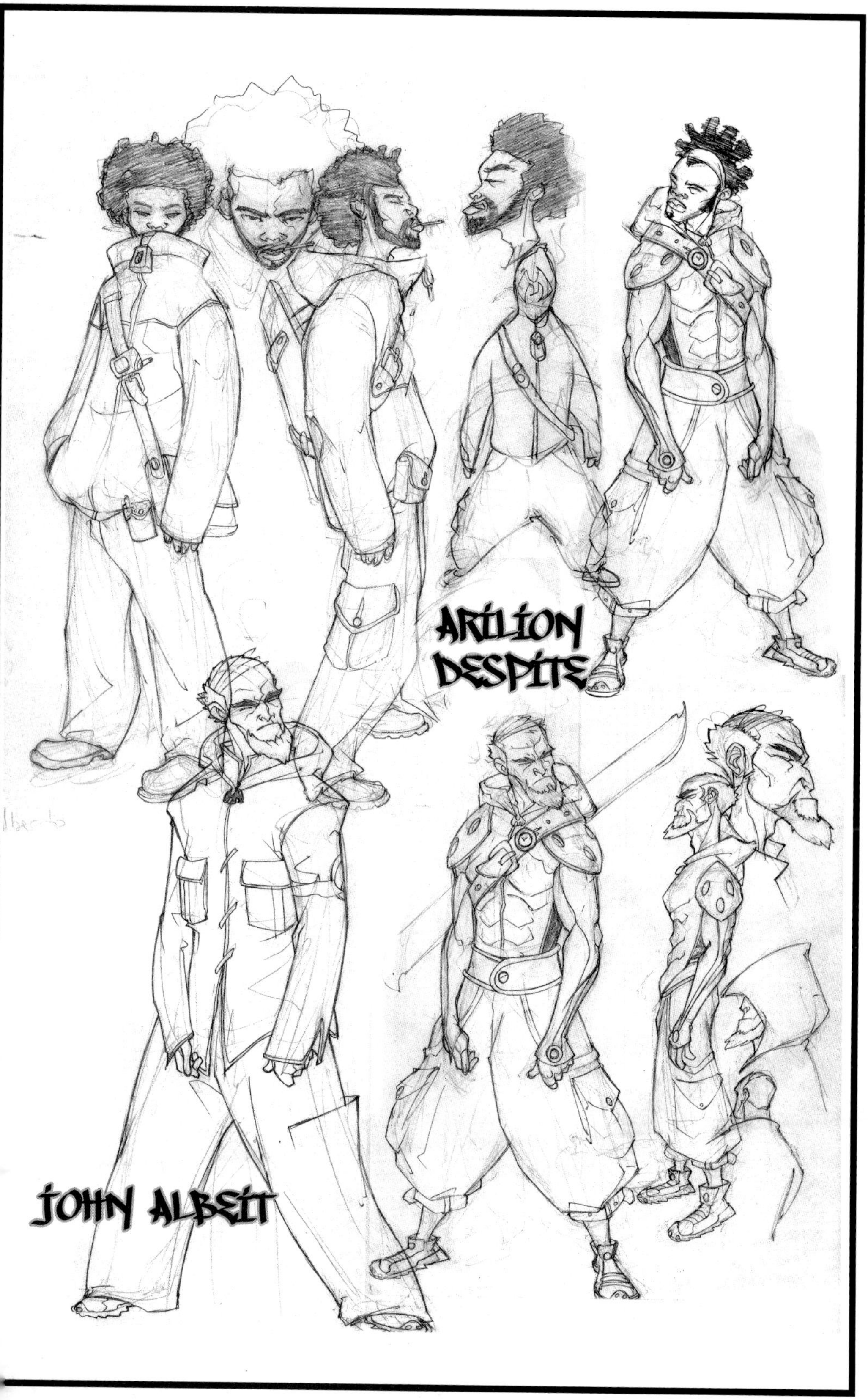
ARILION DESPITE
JOHN ALBEIT

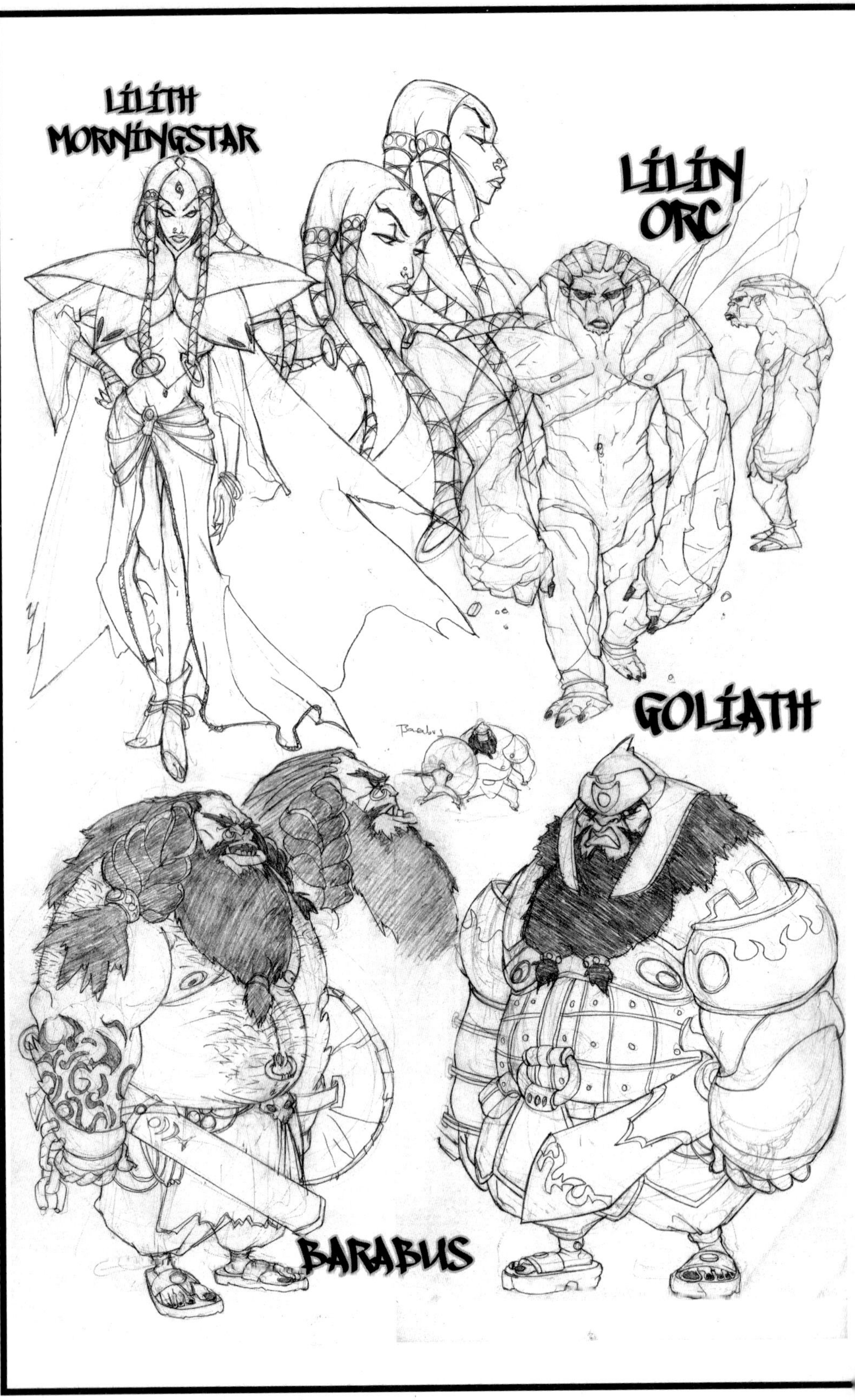
LÍLÍTH MORNÍNGSTAR
LÍLÍN ORC
GOLÍATH
Barabus
BARABUS

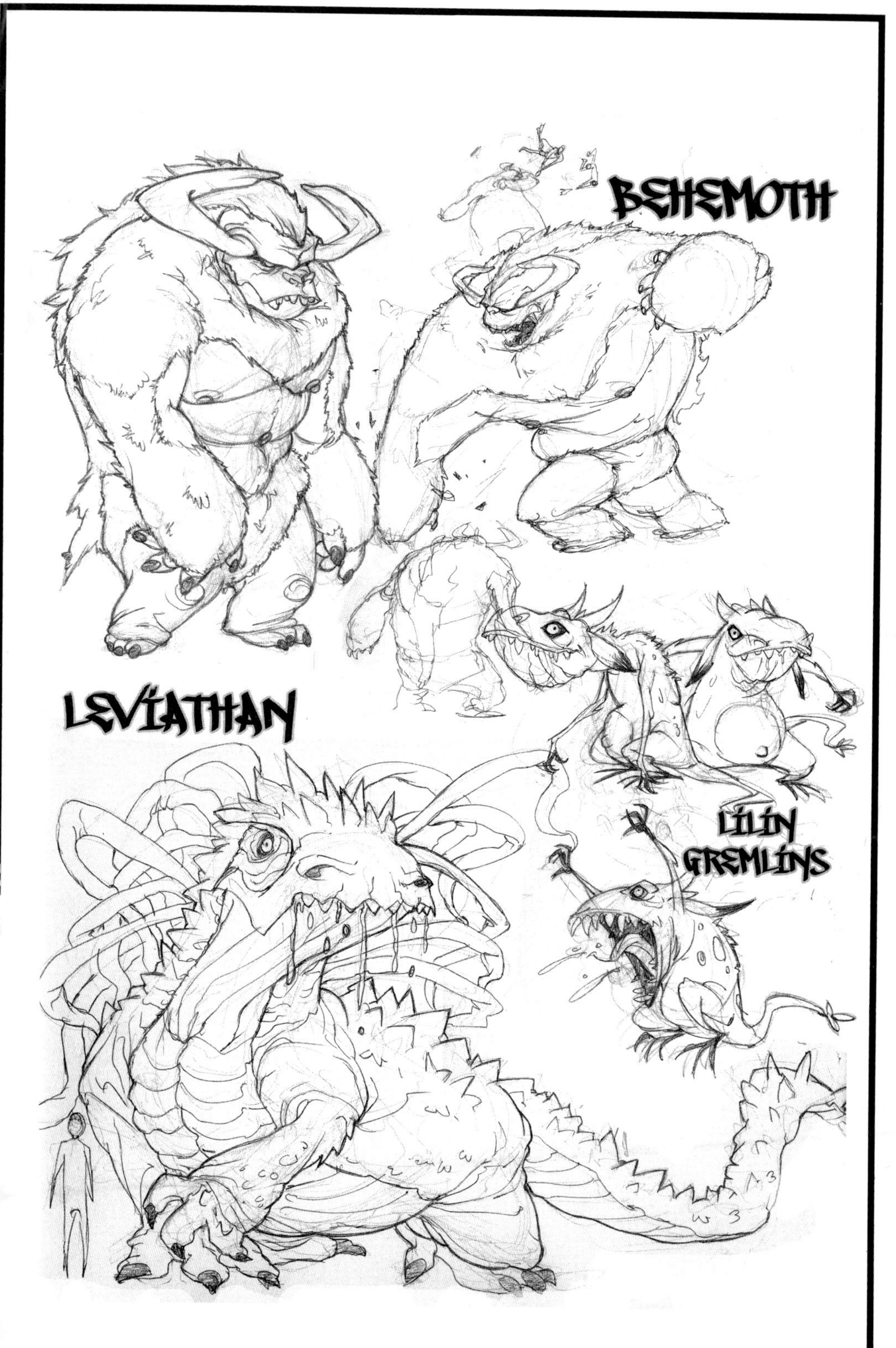
BEHEMOTH
LEVIATHAN
LILIN
GREMLINS